B43 117 273 5 _____ MSC __

D0767647

ROTHERHAM LIBRARY & INFORMATION SERVICES

This book must be returned by the date specified at the time of issue
as the DATE DUE FOR RETURN.
The loan may be extended (personally, by post or telephone) for a
further period if the book is not required by another reader, by quoting
the above number / author / title.

LIS7a

ROTHERHAM LIBRARY & INFORMATION SERVICES	
B48 117278 5	
Askews	
J940.3	£4.99
	R00042163

Text, copyright © Bob Fowke 2002

Illustrations, copyright © Andrew Mee 2002

The right of Bob Fowke to be identified as the author of the work has been asserted by him in accordance with the Copyright, Designs and Patents Act 1988.

Produced by Fowke & Co. for Hodder Children's Books

Published by Hodder Children's Books 2003

0 340 85186 4

10 9 8 7 6 5 4 3 2 1

All rights reserved. No part of this publication may be reproduced, stored in a retrieval system, or transmitted, in any form or by any means, without the prior written permission of the publisher, nor be otherwise circulated in any form of binding or cover other than that in which it is published and without a similar condition being imposed on the subsequent purchaser.

Hodder Children's Books
a division of Hodder Headline Limited
338 Euston Road
London NW1 3BH

Printed and bound in Great Britain by Bookmarque Ltd, Croydon, Surrey
A Catalogue record for this book is available from the British Library

Who? What? When? World War I

By Bob Fowke

With drawings by Andrew Mee

Hodder Children's Books

a division of Hodder Headline Limited

Plea for forgiveness

World War I of 1914-18 was the most terrible war which has ever been fought, except possibly for World War II, which followed twenty-one years later. It was fought between two groups of countries: the *Allies*, including Britain, France and Russia on one side and the *Central Powers*, including Germany and Austria-Hungary, on the other side. The Allies won and the Central Powers lost. It's said that an entire generation of young men died in the conflict. An exaggeration, but nevertheless the bodies of the dead, if laid head to toe, would have stretched for 15,084 kilometres (9,375 miles) - nearly halfway round the world.

It's hard to make head or tail of such a huge disaster. A library of books would not be enough to describe the horror of it all - and a library of books has indeed been written. This book takes the most important bits, the bits you need to know about for your studies or simply if you want to grasp the basics of what happened. Pity the poor author who had to decide what those important bits are, and forgive him if he's left out things or people that you think should be in.

Bob Fowke

royalty

 army life

 poets and writers

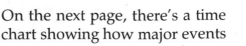 armies and soldiers

weapons

How to read this book

 battles

Entries are listed alphabetically. If you prefer, you can find which page someone or something is on by looking in the index starting on page 123.

 angels

 friends

Words followed by* - you can look up what they mean in the glossary on page 122.

 heroes

 doctors and nurses

Names in **bold** in the text are of people who have their own entry. The little number in the margin beside them shows which page you'll find them on.

 civilians

 generals

 strategies

politicians

On the next page, there's a time chart showing how major events in the war were connected.

rebels

 transport

women

 admirals

 flying machines

  ships

When?

28 June 1914: Assassination of Austrian Archduke Franz Ferdinand in Sarajevo - the spark which starts the war.

23 August 1914: Battle of Mons. Germans and British fight for the first time.

22-29 August 1914: Battle of Tannenberg. Hindenburg and Ludendorff become German heroes.

6-12 September 1914: First Battle of the Marne. Paris is saved and the Germans are stopped.

15 October - 14 November 1914: First Battle of Ypres in southern Belgium. The Germans have switched their main attack away from the Paris region.

7 May 1915: *Lusitania* sunk by German submarine - which angers many Americans.

21 February - December 1916: Battle of Verdun. Germans try to crush French resistance and fail.

24 April - 1 May 1916: Easter Rising. Irish rebels seize the centre of Dublin.

30 May 1916: Battle of Jutland. British and German fleets meet in the only major sea battle of the war.

23 June - 18 November 1916: First Battle of the Somme. Mainly British attempt to draw German pressure away from Verdun. Huge losses sadden the British public.

February 1917: *Russian Revolution - takes Russia out of the war.*

2 April 1917: America joins the war on the side of the Allies.

April - May 1917: Disastrous Nivelle Offensive. Begins with the battles of Chemin des Dames and of Arras.

31 July - 6 November 1917: Third Battle of Ypres. The British try to break through German lines in Belgium.

20 November - 7 December 1917: Battle of Cambrai. Tanks used successfully for the first time.

21 March - 5 April 1918: Kaiserschlacht. Major German offensive before Americans arrive in force. It grinds to a halt.

11 November 1918: Armistice signed by German and Allied representatives.

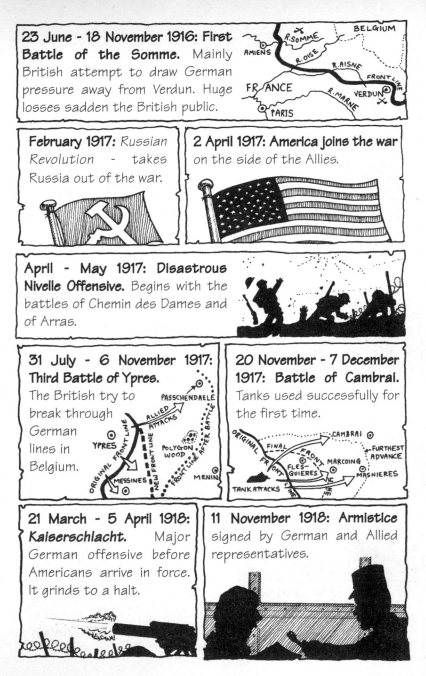

 # airships ✦

highly inflammable, high-flying machines

17 **Balloons** float in the air because the gas or hot air in the balloon is lighter than the air around it. They drift with the wind which makes them unreliable as a form of transport. An *airship* is basically a balloon which can be steered. The first airship was invented by the Frenchman Henri Giffard in 1852 and was called a 'dirigible' from the French *diriger* to steer. In July 1900, the German Count Ferdinand von Zeppelin launched an improved dirigible. The hydrogen gas in the 'balloon' was contained in a light, rigid framework. *Zeppelins* looked like huge, shiny cigars.

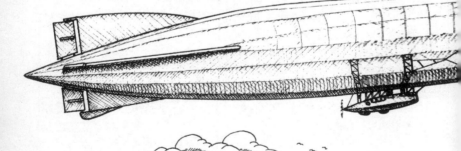

During World War I, airships were used by both sides for observation. The Germans also used them for bombing. The first attack on Britain came in January 1915 when two airships appeared over East Anglia, so high up that they looked 'like bright silver insects'. Four people were killed. Bombing raids on London and Paris and other places in France and England soon followed.

Airships could fly higher than planes of the period and carried a lot more bombs. (The X-type Zeppelin could reach a height of 7,000 metres - 4.35 miles.) They were beautiful to look at and flew so lazily that people would come out of their houses to watch them drift by - but they made a huge, slow target for gunners and defending **planes**. When hit, the gas would burn up almost instantly. The German army stopped using them over battlefields in 1916, after three out of four were shot down over **Verdun**, France. Airship bombing raids against Britain continued on and off almost to the end of the war.

27 Aisne, Second Battle of *see* **Chemin des Dames, Battle of**

🜲 Albert I, King of Belgium
brave king who led his country's army

1875-1934

On 2 August 1914, at the very outbreak of war, the German army demanded free passage to France across Belgium soil - Albert I, King of Belgium, refused. The Germans invaded two days later. Under Albert's brave leadership the small Belgian army fought back, but they were forced to retreat, first to Antwerp in the west and then into Flanders in the south-west of Belgium, the only part of the country which was never occupied by the Germans during the war.

Albert stayed with his men and in 1918 he led a joint French/Belgium army back into Belgium, re-entering Brussels, the capital, on 22 November 1918. He finally died of a fall when rock climbing in the Ardennes, having governed his country well for another sixteen years.

Allenby, General Sir Edmund 'The Bull'

he fought in Palestine

1861-1936

General Allenby was a large man, known as 'the Bull' by his fellow officers because he was so strong. At the start of the war he was a cavalry commander with the **British Expeditionary Force** in France. In 1917, he was sent to lead the British forces fighting the Turks in the Middle East. At that time, most of the Middle East was still a part of the Turkish Empire - and Turkey was an ally of Germany.

With Allenby in command, the British fought their way north across Palestine from their base in Egypt. The Turks were no match for the British, who were aided throughout by Arab troops in revolt against their Turkish rulers. (The British hero, **T.E. Lawrence** helped to organise the Arabs.) Allenby was the last general ever to use massed cavalry effectively. In the

conditions of the Middle East, they were surprisingly
66 good against **machine guns** if they charged fast
enough. The British captured Jerusalem in December
29 1917. On **Churchill's** advice, Allenby entered the city
on foot so as not to look like Jesus, who had once
entered it on a donkey.

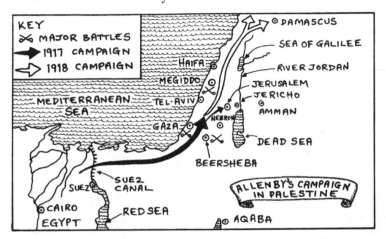

KEY
✖ MAJOR BATTLES
➡ 1917 CAMPAIGN
⟹ 1918 CAMPAIGN

DAMASCUS
SEA OF GALILEE
HAIFA
RIVER JORDAN
MEGIDDO
JERUSALEM
JERICHO
MEDITERRANEAN SEA
TEL-AVIV
AMMAN
HEBRON
GAZA
DEAD SEA
BEERSHEBA
SUEZ CANAL
SUEZ
ALLENBY'S CAMPAIGN IN PALESTINE
CAIRO
EGYPT
RED SEA
AQABA

By the victorious end of the campaign, in October
1918, Allenby's men had fought their way across 500
miles of enemy territory. They took 65,000 prisoners,
including 3,400 Germans and Austrians.

Allies
friends - for a while

Allied countries, or *allies*, agree to help each other if
any one of them comes under attack. 'Allies' with a
capital 'A' is the name given to the group of countries
which fought the Germans and their friends (called
27 the **Central Powers**) during World War I. The Allies
consisted of: Britain, France, Greece, Portugal,
Belgium, Italy, Serbia, Japan and Russia. America
joined later, in 1917.

Angels of Mons
bowmen in the sky

In August 1914, it was widely believed that British troops retreating from the **Battle of Mons** were protected by the ghosts of medieval English bowmen, bowmen who had fought at the Battle of Crécy in 1346. It was said that British soldiers saw the ghosts of the bowmen looming above the battlefield.

Armistice
agreement to pack it in

An armistice is an agreement by both sides in a war to stop fighting. Usually there's an armistice first and then detailed peace negotiations get started. The final Armistice of World War I, that between Germany and the **Allies**, came into effect at 11.00 on 11 November 1918 - the eleventh hour of the eleventh day of the eleventh month. It was signed in a railway carriage in the forest of Compiègne in northern France by **Marshal Foch** and two representatives of the German government. Now, at 11.00 on 11 November each year, called 'Armistice Day' - the 'Day of Remembrance', we all keep two minute's silence in memory of the brave souls who died fighting in World War I and in the wars which have come after. People wear red paper poppies in memory of the poppies which grew in the waste of 72 **no man's land**.

✗ Arras, Battle of
offensive start to an offensive

SPRING 1917

The Battle of Arras came at the start of the 72 catastrophic Nivelle Offensive, launched by **General Nivelle**, who believed that the Germans were 11 weakening and that the **Allies** could win if they attacked hard enough. The British had dug tunnels close up to the German lines from caves and sewers beneath the town of Arras so the attacking troops could cover some of the distance towards the German trenches in safety. However, due to the 14 British **artillery** bombardment, the Germans had been given plenty of warning of the attack. When the British soldiers came out of the tunnels, they were 66 mown down by German **machine guns**.

The battle was extremely bloody. North of Arras, the Canadian Corps lost 14,000 men while capturing the vital vantage point of Vimy Ridge. Fighting continued, off and on, into late May. By that time, the 19 **British Expeditionary Force** had lost 150,000 men against 100,000 Germans - thought to be a good 'ratio of **attrition**' by many of the British top brass for an attack against well-defended enemy positions.

 artillery

big guns and how they were handled

Big guns dominated the battlefields of World War I. Generals on both sides believed that it was vital to 'soften up' the enemy with an artillery barrage, known as a 'preliminary bombardment', before any general infantry attack. Such barrages were often huge affairs. Before the attack on Messines in mid-1917, the British launched a two week barrage with 2,500 guns and fired 3.5 million shells. During such a barrage the sky was literally thick with flying metal.

The non-stop noise of the big guns was almost as terrifying as the explosion of their shells. The gunners themselves frequently suffered from

BRITISH
'3 - POUNDER'
GUN

bleeding ears and even from concussion because of it. The biggest guns, such as the German gun *Big Bertha*, could shoot huge shells of up to 120 kg over distances of up to 122 km (76 miles). Due to their weight, big guns were very difficult to move forward through the wasteland of mud and shell craters which they themselves created. Attacks often ran out of steam because the guns got left behind.

Unfortunately, 'preliminary bombardment' meant that there could be no surprise attacks. What tended to happen was that the enemy hid in their underground bunkers until the barrage was over. Then, once the infantry attack started, the enemy came out of their bunkers, still alive and ready to fight back. Meanwhile, the artillery shells had churned the ground into a sea of mud for the poor old attacking infantry to wade through. Later in the war, gunners developed the tactic of 'rolling artillery fire': as the attacking soldiers moved forward, shells from their own artillery were fired over their heads from behind them, aimed to explode continuously about two hundred yards ahead of the soldiers as they advanced. This was meant to force the enemy to keep their heads down and to protect the attackers from enemy fire.

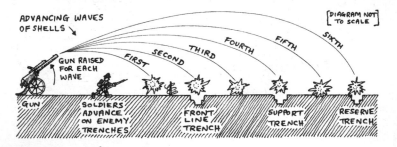

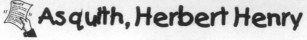# Asquith, Herbert Henry

1852-1928

Herbert Asquith was Prime Minister of Great Britain 58 when war broke out. He appointed **General Kitchener** to be War Minister. He was forced from 62 power by **Lloyd George** on 7 December 1916 after 97 the terrible British losses at the **Battle of the Somme**.

# attrition
the bitter end

A war of *attrition* is a war in which the two sides slug it out until one or the other can go on no longer. In World War I, a 'policy of attrition' was believed in by 111 many top commanders on both sides. Before **Verdun** for instance, German commanders decided that they would have to 'bleed France white'. In other words: Germany had more men than France so France would have to give up first. If necessary, war would be over when the last German killed the last Frenchman. Or, as Sir William Robertson, a British general, is supposed to have said: the war would be over when there were two British soldiers and one German left in the field.

85
43
94 **Balkans** *see* **Salonika**, **Gallipoli** and **side shows**

balloons
but not the birthday kind

Observation balloons were first used in warfare by the French in 1793, during the Napoleonic wars. They were very useful for seeing behind enemy lines and they were used for the same purpose in World War I. An observer with a map and telescope would be lifted up in the basket and from there he made notes of enemy positions, passing on his information to the ground either by flag signals or by radio. The balloon was tethered to the ground by a rope.

The observer in his balloon, or 'blimp' as they were known in World War I, was a 'sitting duck' when it came to enemy fire and balloonists had to be very brave men. The balloons themselves were difficult to shoot down since bullets tended to whiz straight through them and out the other side without doing too much damage - the balloon could usually be lowered to safety before it lost too much air.

In World War I, balloons were especially useful for directing artillery fire, since gunners were too far away from their targets to see where their shells landed. Two or three balloons acting together could give the gunners accurate map coordinates for the positions of exploding shells. The gunners could then adjust their aim accordingly. Balloons towed above ships were also useful at sea for spotting enemy submarines.

19 BEF *see* **British Expeditionary Force**

⊗ blackout
not a light to be seen

The first attacks on Britain by long-distance German bombers came in 1916. There was no radio navigation so the bombers had to rely on their eyes to guide them. To make things as difficult as possible for the German bombers, there was a total *blackout* across Britain. All windows were covered and no street lights were lit. It was very hard for the bombers to know when they were over open country and when they were over built-up areas with targets such as armament factories.

Bolsheviks
they took Russia out of the war

In February 1917, in St. Petersburg, then the Russian capital, **Czar Nicholas II** of Russia was overthrown in a revolution led by angry soldiers and sailors. Meanwhile at the front, Russian soldiers refused to obey their officers and the Russian army stopped fighting. The *Bolsheviks*, the name means 'members of the majority' in Russian, were a revolutionary communist* party. They soon became the most powerful political party in Russia, mainly because they called for their country to pull out of the war altogether, which was what many Russians wanted. Led by Vladimir Ilyich Lenin, the Bolsheviks swept aside all opposition and in October they seized power in an armed coup. They then negotiated a peace treaty with the Germans at the war-damaged town of Brest-Litovsk, then the eastern German headquarters (signed 3 March 1918).

British Expeditionary Force (BEF)
the British army in western Europe

Back in 1908, Britain's small, regular army was reorganised. Instead of preparing for wars in far flung corners of the British Empire, its main job was now to be as an 'expeditionary force' to the continent

19

of Europe if Germans should attack France - which was a possibility even then.

When war did break out, this 'British Expeditionary Force' of professional soldiers, 'BEF' for short, was sent to Belgium almost immediately. It was made up of just four infantry divisions and one cavalry division, under the command of **Sir John French**, and totalled about 120,000 men in all.

The BEF suffered heavy losses at the hand of the much larger German army. However, within a year it was reinforced by the newly recruited '**Kitchener armies**', and by the end of the war it was probably the most powerful and best-armed army in the world. Between 1914 and 1918, the BEF suffered nearly 3 million casualties, including 900,000 dead. BEF is also the name given to British forces in France in World War II.

British Legion
ex-servicemen's society

When World War I was finally over, British ex-servicemen had many problems, including disability due to war wounds and unemployment due to lack of jobs. The British Legion was formed in 1921.

Through the British Legion, ex-servicemen were better able to ask government and the public for help and to help each other. **Douglas Haig** helped to set it up and was its first president. From that day to this, the Legion has helped British ex-servicemen of many wars, and there are British Legion social clubs all over the country.

47

♀ ✎ Brittain, Vera ☞

youthful writer of wartime experiences

1893-1970

Vera Brittain wrote her most famous book, *Testament of Youth*, after World War I ended. It was published in 1933. The book describes her experiences in the period leading up to and during the war. During the war, she was a **VAD** and served as a nurse in France and Malta. Meanwhile, one by one, her friends, her clever fiancé Roland Leighton and finally her much loved, younger brother Edward were all killed. Such terrible losses happened to thousands of young women during the war but Vera was able to write about them with heart-breaking honesty. She became a pacifist* because she was horrified by the waste of young lives. As she put it in her book:

110

> *The world was mad and we were all victims.*

Brooke, Rupert

handsome poet who died young

1887-1915

Rupert Brooke was handsome and charming and a poet: 'a creature on whom the gods had smiled their brightest' as the American writer Henry James described him. He became an officer in the Royal Naval Division at the outbreak of war in 1914 and was a member of the British expedition to save Antwerp from the Germans that same year. In Belgium he saw the horror of the German occupation but died before he had a chance to see the even worse horrors of the trenches in France. Because of this, his war poems are more patriotic and less critical of the war than the work of other war poets such as **Siegfried Sassoon** and **Wilfrid Owen**. Rupert died of blood poisoning while on board a troop ship bound for **Gallipoli**. His most famous war poem speaks of his love of England:

87
73

43

> *If I should die, think only this of me:*
> *That there's some corner of a foreign field*
> *That is for ever England. There shall be*
> *In that rich earth a richer dust concealed;*
> *A dust whom England bore, shaped, made aware ...*

Brusilov, General Aleksey
Russian who won by surprise

1853-1926

In March 1916, Aleksey Brusilov was made commander of four Russian armies fighting the Austrians in south-west Russia. Instead of waiting for massive reinforcements in order to build up a huge force in a narrow part of the front (standard tactics for the Russians), he chose to attack all along the front using surprise as his main weapon. The 'Brusilov Offensive' of June 1916 was a brilliant success. By August when the offensive finally petered out, the Russians had captured 375,000 Austrian prisoners.

Cambrai, Battle of
when tanks took over

At dawn on 20 November 1917, German troops manning the trenches of the **Hindenburg Line** to the west of the town of Cambrai in northern France were woken by the roar of primitive engines. Then 378 vast, dinosaur-like machines rolled out of the early morning mist towards them. The attack was a total

48

102 surprise. The **tanks**, because that's what they were, had been hidden beneath trees and in burned-out buildings behind the British lines, out of sight of German planes and balloons. They were almost unstoppable and carried huge bundles of sticks which they dropped into the German trenches so that they could roll over them.

Cambrai was the first mass tank attack of the war,
indeed of any war. Cambrai was chosen because the
chalk downland was perfect tank country. Before the
big attack, there was no preliminary bombardment
14 by **artillery** so the ground was still firm for the tanks
to travel over. By late afternoon, they'd gained six
kilometres of ground for the loss of very few men. It
was a breakthrough by the standards of World War I
- and a turning point in the war. Thanks to tanks, at
long last *attackers* had protection from the machine
guns of *defenders*.

Unfortunately, at Cambrai the tanks didn't have enough back-up to hold onto their gains. Fierce fighting went on until 30 November when the Germans counter-attacked. By 7 December, the two sides were roughly back where they started - except that the British had lost about 45,000 men and the Germans slightly more.

Casement, Sir Roger David
diplomatic Irish freedom fighter
1864-1916

Sir Roger Casement was a successful British diplomat. He was also a Protestant Irishman at a time when all of Ireland was still ruled by Britain. Unlike most British diplomats, Casement believed in total Irish independence. When the war started, he sailed to Germany and asked the Germans for guns and

36 ammunition for the planned '**Easter Rising**' by Irish nationalists against the British. The Germans agreed

to send a shipload of German arms to Dublin and Casement travelled home on a German submarine. But the plot was known about by British agents. Casement was arrested on landing in Ireland. He was hanged in Pentonville prison on 3 August 1916.

causes of the war
why so many countries started fighting

In the years leading up to 1914, the countries of Europe were tied up in two grand alliances

11 (groupings of friendly countries). The **Allies**, including Britain and France, were on one side, and

27 the **Central Powers**, including Germany and Austria, were on the other side. This was dangerous because if any two countries from either side started fighting,

all the other countries would get pulled in. And that's roughly what happened. Briefly:

28 July: Austria declared war on Serbia.
1 August: Germany declared war on Russia (because Russia was about to come to the aid of the Serbs against Germany's ally Austria).
3 August: Germany declared war on France (which was about to come to the aid of its ally Russia).
4 August: Germany invaded neutral Belgium en route to France.
4 August: Britain declared war on Germany (in aid of Britain's ally France and of neutral Belgium).

Cavell, Edith Louisa
nurse and heroine
1865-1915

Edith Cavell was an English nurse who was working in Brussels when World War I broke out. She carried on working after the Germans captured the city and treated wounded Germans as well as Belgian and British soldiers cut off by the German advance. But she also helped many Belgian and British soldiers to escape from German-occupied territory. The Germans found out about this and arrested her. After nine weeks solitary confinement, she confessed and, after a short trial, she was shot. The British, who never executed women spies, were shocked.

Central Powers

Central Powers is the name given to Germany and the countries which fought on Germany's side in World War I. They were: Germany, the Austro-Hungarian Empire, Bulgaria, Romania and Turkey.

Chemin des Dames, Battle of
✂ a road and a battle

On the morning of 16 April 1917, the French army launched a massive attack on the newly-built **Hindenburg Line**. Chemin des Dames is the name of a road to the north of Rheims where some of the fiercest fighting took place. The battle, also called the Second Battle of the Aisne, had been planned by the French Commander-in-Chief, **General Robert Nivelle**, who believed that 'great violence with great mass' could win the war. More than a million French soldiers were thrown into the fight, backed up by 7,000 guns. Like the rest of Nivelle's offensive, it was an utter disaster. 40,000 French soldiers died on the first day alone. By the end of the battle on 9 May, 355,000 men had died, including 187,000 Frenchmen - for a few hundred metres of land.

48

72

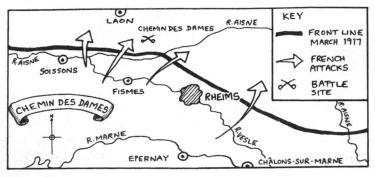

French soldiers were so disgusted by the disaster that mutinies broke out in several regiments. The men understandably refused to leave their trenches when ordered to attack. General Nivelle was sacked from his position as French Commander-in-Chief within a week of the end of the battle and it was left to his 75 successor **General Pétain** to sort out the mess.

Christmas Truce
when enemies made friends

During their training, soldiers on both sides were taught to hate each other, but hatred tended not to last for very long in the conditions of the western 107 front. Often the two opposing lines of **trenches** were less than twenty metres away from each other; sometimes they even ran through the same ruined houses. The men could hear each other sneeze. It didn't take long for soldiers on both sides to realise that their enemies were men very much like themselves. Often they would shout jokes and messages to each other, although this was always frowned on by the top brass. On Christmas Day 1914, the war broke down completely. German and British 72 soldiers spilled out of their trenches into **no man's land**. They gave each other presents, there was a joint burial service and even a football game.

You can't fight a war if the soldiers make friends with each other. The generals were very cross and there were no more Christmas truces.

 # Churchill, Winston
'Winnie'
plucky politician who never gave up
1874-1965

Winston Churchill is most famous for his role as Prime Minister of Britain during World War II, but he was also a very important leader during World War I. In 1914, as First Lord of the Admiralty at the very start of the war, he sailed to Belgium and seized control of the defence of Antwerp with absolutely no regard for his own safety.

In February 1915 he set up a tank committee to develop tanks - for the army! Churchill was the only top leader who guessed how useful tanks would be.

62
16
Like **Lloyd George**, Churchill was sickened by trench warfare. He asked Prime Minister **Asquith**:

Are there not other alternatives than sending out armies to chew barbed wire in Flanders?

43
To reduce losses in France, Churchill dreamt up the idea of an expedition to the **Dardanelles**, in modern

Turkey, then an ally of Germany, hoping that the Dardanelles would be the back door to victory in Europe. The expedition turned out to be a bloody failure and Churchill took the blame. He left the Admiralty and for a while took command of a battalion of soldiers in France. In December 1916, his old friend Lloyd George became Prime Minister, and in July 1917 Churchill was made Minister of Munitions, in charge of the manufacture of ammunition. He did the job with his usual incredible energy. His habit was to sleep in the afternoons and then work on through the night while lesser men rested. Churchill could never be accused of being lazy.

Clemenceau, Georges
French Prime Minister who fought to win
1841-1929

In November 1916, France was on its knees as a result of the war. A fighter like Clemenceau was needed if France was to stay in the war. He was made Prime Minister (for the second time, he was Prime Minister

1906-9 as well) by President Poincaré, and promised to continue fighting:

... to the last quarter hour, for the last quarter hour will be ours.

Clemenceau was ruthless with pacifists and anyone who suggested that France might lose. When the war was over he was equally ruthless in making sure that Germany paid 'reparations' for starting it. But he was also a cultured man. He had championed the French Impressionist painters in the 1870s, and had been a leader of the left-wing Paris Commune in 1871. When he retired from government in 1920, he lived on for another nine years, travelling and writing.

conscientious objectors ⊘
they refused to fight

Some people thought it was wrong to fight in the war. They were called *'conscientious objectors'*, also 'conchies' and 'pasty faces'. They weren't popular. 'Fatty degeneration of the soul' was how one newspaper described their principles, and one prison chaplain said he thought that the conchies in his prison ought to be drowned! Conchies were **conscripted** into the war effort just the same. Some

33

were forced to join the army, but there were plenty of war jobs which didn't involve fighting. Many conchies became medical orderlies or ambulance drivers and rescued wounded men under enemy fire.

1916 'COMMER' AMBULANCE

'Absolute conscientious objectors' were conchies with knobs on. They refused to have anything at all to do with the war. They wouldn't even drive ambulances. Often such people were members of religious sects such as the Jehovah's Witnesses. 6,000 spent the war in British prisons and seventy of them died in prison as a result of the treatment they received. Others were sent to mental hospitals.

Conchies kept their spirits up by publishing their own newspaper, the *Dreadnought*. It was the 87 *Dreadnought* which first published **Siegfried Sassoon's** famous letter:

I believe the war is being deliberately prolonged by those who have the power to end it ...

conscription
forced to fight

Conscription means that fit men (and sometimes women too nowadays) have to join the armed services, whether they want to or not, by order of the government. At the start of the war, France, Germany, Austria and Russia all had huge armies of conscript soldiers. Britain was the only major European power which had no conscription and only a small, professional army of voluntary soldiers.

Even after the war started, the British government had no need to conscript men. So many joined up voluntarily that the government had more soldiers than it knew what to do with - 2.6 million volunteered by January 1916. But eventually, even 2.6 million wasn't enough. Men died by the thousand on the battlefields of France and the

16

government ran out of volunteers. In January 1916, the Military Service Acts were passed by the **Asquith** government and 2.3 million more men were conscripted into the army to bring it up to strength.

convoys

ships seeking safety in numbers

Part of Germany's war plan was to starve Britain into

99 giving in. For most of the war German **submarines** picked off British merchant shipping almost at will.

By 1917 they were sinking 630,000 tons of Allied shipping *per month*.

29
62 The answer, as **Winston Churchill, Lloyd George** and many junior officers in the Royal Navy kept saying, was *convoys*: group the merchant ships together into convoys and protect the convoys with warships. Senior officers in the navy resisted this idea for a long time. Among other things, they believed that because convoys must steam at the speed of their slowest ship, the naval escorts would become sitting ducks for submarines to aim at.

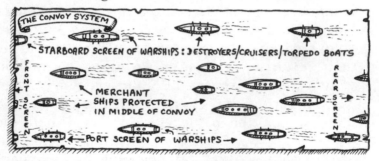

In actual fact convoys had two advantages:

> 1. Merchant ships were no longer scattered all over the oceans. This meant that U-boats could no longer cruise at random and expect to bump into their prey.
> 2. If a U-boat attacked a convoy, it might only get in one shot. After that it had to dive quickly before the naval escort ships could sink it.

Convoys were finally introduced by a reluctant navy in February 1917, by the new Lloyd George government. In a trial involving British coal ships bound for France, only nine out of 4,000 ships were sunk. Soon convoys were being widely used. Allied shipping losses fell from 25% in April 1917 to 1% by December 1917.

43 Dardanelles *see* **Gallipoli**

⊘ doing your bit
what civilians* did to help

Everyone in Britain was expected to 'do their bit' for the war effort. Women formed clubs to knit socks and other things for the soldiers. 'Feed the guns' campaigns raised money for tanks and ammunition through jumble sales and gifts. Children collected silver paper, wool and rags for the same purpose. And most people grew food in gardens or allotments. Gardens, tennis courts and parks were all 47 dug up and planted with vegetables. **King George** grew potatoes at Buckingham Palace.

Taking holidays was thought to be unpatriotic and bank holidays became a thing of the past. It was wise to *look* like you were doing your bit even if you weren't. The rich walked around in trousers with baggy knees and frayed hems so as not to be criticised for wasting materials.

107 **dugouts** *see* **trenches**

Easter Rising
Irish rebellion around a post office

In 1914, when World War I started, Ireland was part of the British Empire. Thousands of Irishmen fought loyally for Britain during the war. But many others wanted their country to be independent. On 24 April 1916, Easter Monday, a group of Irish nationalists captured Dublin's central post office and several other buildings in the city and declared a provisional, independent Irish government.

Unfortunately for them, the British authorities had had word of the uprising. On 21 April they had
25 arrested **Sir Roger Casement** on his way back from a mission to Germany to collect arms for the rebels.

The *Easter Rising* was put down by British troops after fierce street fighting in which three hundred people died. The rebels surrendered on 1 May. Fourteen of the rebel leaders were executed by the British authorities - executions which shocked many Irish people, making them more anti-British than they'd been before. It was partly due to the Easter Rising that the Irish Free State was finally established on 6 December 1921.

 Eastern Front

The Eastern Front was the huge area of eastern Europe where the war was fought between Germany and Austria-Hungary on one side and the Russians on the other side. It stretched from the Baltic Sea in the north to the Black Sea in the south.

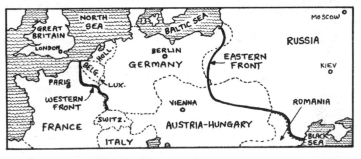

 Etaples
tough training camp in France

58 When **Herbert Kitchener** called for volunteers for his new 'Kitchener' armies in 1914, thousands rushed to join. By January 1916, 2.6 million men had joined up. Most of these raw recruits knew nothing about soldiering, which caused huge problems for the army authorities who had to train them. The men

were trained first in Britain and, after they'd been shipped over to France, at a huge training camp near Etaples, a small town in northern France about fifteen miles south of Boulogne.

Etaples, or 'Eat-Apples' as the men called it, was a very tough place. Bullying sergeant majors forced the men to march for hours in the 'Bull Ring', an enormous parade ground. Hard punishments were dished out to anyone who broke the rules. An odd way to treat men who had after all *volunteered* to fight for their country.

YOU 'ORRIBLE LITTLE MAN! WHAT ARE YOU?

AN 'ORRIBLE LITTLE MAN, SIR!

Falkenhayn, General Erich von
German general who fell from favour
1861-1922

VERDAMMT!

VERDUN
DIE VERLUSTLISTE

50

111

General Falkenhayn was Chief of Staff of the German army at the start of World War I. He was replaced by **Hindenburg** in August 1916 following the terrible failure of the German attacks on **Verdun**. Later in the war, he took command of German operations in Turkey and Palestine. In Palestine he was soundly defeated by the British under **General Allenby**.

10

94 **Far East** *see* **side shows**

field hospitals
something for suffering soldiers

Both sides in the war set up mobile hospitals near to the front to treat the thousands of men who were wounded in action. The wounded were far more likely to bleed to death or die in some other way if they had to be carried a long way behind the lines before they could be treated. Field hospitals for both sides were usually set up in deserted buildings taken over for the purpose, or in canvas tents.

Many of the nurses who worked in the field hospitals were members of the **Voluntary Aid Detachments**, or VADs, well brought-up middle class girls who had led very sheltered lives until the war began. The blood, mess and suffering came as a terrible shock to most of them.

Fisher, Admiral John
sea dog who served the navy

1841-1920

Admiral John Fisher was an old-time sea dog. He had the energy of a rocket, charm by the bucketful and no respect for stuffy tradition in the (very traditional)

Royal Navy. As First Sea Lord (1903-10) he had totally transformed the Navy. He sacked senior officers who weren't up to the job and stripped the navy of smaller, older ships. He believed in new technology, which in those days meant the three 'Ts': telegraph, turbine engines and torpedoes. He introduced the *Dreadnought*, the first 'big gun' battleship.

29 **Winston Churchill**, as First Lord of the Admiralty, recalled Fisher from retirement in October 1914. The two men worked well together for a while, but they
43 disagreed about the **Dardanelles** expedition. Fisher resigned on 15 May 1915. He finished the war as head of the 'Board of Inventions', a job after his own heart since it was about introducing new technology to the armed forces.

flu epidemic
serious sickness which swept the world

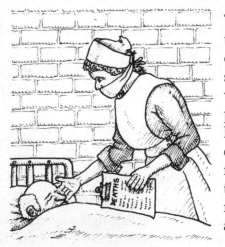

Towards the end of the war a very dangerous type of flu swept round the world. 27 million people are said to have died in the epidemic within a few months - more than three times the number who died as a result of the war.

🎖️ Foch, Marshal Ferdinand

French general who led the Allies

1851-1929

Ferdinand Foch believed in the 'offensive spirit' - that armies have the best chance of winning if they attack whenever possible. In April 1918, he became Allied Supreme Commander, commanding both the French and British armies. It was Foch who commanded the final Allied victory and Foch who accepted the German surrender and plea for an **armistice** in a railway carriage at Compiègne on 9 November. After the war, he was showered with honours. He's buried near to Napoleon at the church of Saint-Louis in Paris.

12

👑 Franz Ferdinand, Archduke of Austria-Este

his death started the war

1863-1914

In 1914, Archduke Ferdinand was heir to the throne of the Austro-Hungarian Empire. On June 28, he and his wife were visiting Sarejevo, the capital of Bosnia, then part of the Empire, when he was shot dead in broad daylight by a young man called Gavrilo Princip. Gavrilo was a member of 'Young Bosnia', an anti-Austrian movement. Bosnia had only recently been swallowed up by the Austrian Empire, but the majority of Bosnians were Serbs like Gavrilo who wanted Bosnia to unite with Serbia. From the

Austrian point of view, if Bosnia was allowed to leave the Austrian Empire, other subject countries might well follow. That was why Austria decided that Serbia had to be punished, and why Austria declared war on Serbia on 28 July 1914 - thus starting World War I.

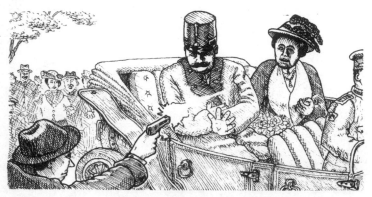

♔ Franz Joseph I, Emperor
ancient Austrian emperor
1830-1916

When World War I started, Franz Joseph had been ruler of the Austro-Hungarian Empire for 47 years. He was eighty-four years old and depressed. In 1889 his then heir had shot himself in a love pact, and in 1898 his beloved wife had been assassinated. When the new heir, his nephew **Archduke Ferdinand**, was assassinated (June 1914) by the young Serb nationalist Gavrilo Princip, Franz declared war on Serbia, thus starting World War I.

41

🎩 French, Field Marshal Sir John

1852-1925

19 John French was commander of the **British Expeditionary Force** at the start of World War I, landing at Boulogne on 14 March 1914. Despite his name, he never found it easy to get on with his
47 French allies. He was replaced by **Douglas Haig** on 4 December 1915.

✗ Gallipoli and the  Dardanelles Expedition

94 (*see also* **side shows**)

second front in the south

The Gallipoli Peninsula runs down one side of the Dardanelles Straits. The Straits lead to Istanbul and are also the gateway to southern Russia. If the Allies could seize control of Gallipoli, Turkey could be cut off from supply from Germany and, at the same time, the Allies would be able to supply Russia from
29 the south. 'Easterners' such as **Winston Churchill**
62 and **Lloyd George**, believed that this might lead to a quicker end to the war - and less lives lost in the killing fields of France.

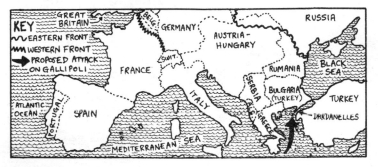

At 11.30 on 18 March 1915, British battleships entered

the Dardanelles, which were heavily defended by Turkish forts perched on the hills of the Asian coast to the south and on the Gallipoli Peninsula to the north. Pounded by heavy guns and forced into a minefield, the fleet was forced to retreat.

Just over a month later, it was time for a second try, with soldiers. A mixed Allied army of more than 90,000 men finally landed on Gallipoli on 25 April, including a large troop of ANZACs (stands for 'Australian and New Zealand Army Corps'). Many were killed or wounded but they gained a toehold on three separate beaches.

That was about all they managed. Despite reinforcements, Gallipoli was a nightmare for the Allies. From day one of the campaign, they were hemmed in by the Turks who defended bravely from high ground. The entire Allied army of 140,000

men and more than 5,000 animals, was taken off in ships of the Royal Navy in January 1916. They left behind them 43,000 British and British Empire soldiers dead and about 5,000 French dead. The Turks lost 65,000. Churchill had dreamed up the Dardanelles Expedition. He was forced to resign as First Sea Lord (May 1916) because of it.

 gas

a poisonous way to fight

Poison gas was a new weapon in World War I. It was first used by the Germans, in the opening stages of the **Second Battle of Ypres** (April 1915) and a number of French north African soldiers were killed. The chlorine gas was released from cylinders (nicknamed 'rogers' by the British) and carried to the unfortunate north Africans on the wind. It was a dirty, greenish-yellow colour and it stained the ground for days afterwards. Further experiments led to phosgene gas which caused deadly choking and then to mustard gas, or 'Yperite', a blistering agent which caused blindness and a painful death.

CRUDE, EARLY (MAY 1915) GAS MASK

Each new development was quickly copied by the Allies. By 1918, both sides were using gas in large quantities, mostly fired at the enemy in special gas-filled shells which were more effective than cylinders - release of gas from cylinders could backfire on the attackers if the wind changed direction. Both Allied and German top brass had plans to fill half of all their new shells with gas for 1919. Mercifully, the war ended first.

To start with, soldiers protected themselves as best they could: socks soaked in urine and held over the nose were quite effective against chlorine, as were cotton wool pads soaked in bicarbonate of soda. Before long, soldiers on both sides carried gas masks. Only 3% of gas victims actually died. The problem was that the remainder suffered from terrible disabilities, such as blindness and damaged lungs. It was public horror at these effects which led to the international ban on chemical weapons, agreed by all major powers in 1925, a ban which is still in force today, although some countries have broken it.

♔ George V, King

king who cared for his country

1863-1936

George V succeeded to the throne of Great Britain on the death of his father Edward VII in 1910 and was king of Britain throughout World War I. He was a patriotic* man. While the war lasted, alcohol was forbidden in the royal household, and from 1917 the royals ate smaller meals to show that they were suffering with their people. In July 1917, George changed the family name from *Hanover*, which is German, to *Windsor* which is English. Windsor has remained the name of the British Royal Family ever since.

GOOD HEAVENS, FATHER! I SHALL STARVE!

EAT UP, EDWARD WINDSOR! WE MUST SHOW SYMPATHY WITH OUR SUBJECTS!

SPRING WATER

107 Going over the top *see* trench warfare

Haig, Field Marshal Sir Douglas

British general people disagree about

1861-1928

Douglas Haig was an efficient man who knew the right people in the right places. He was married to a former lady-in-waiting to the Queen. In 1914, when the **British Expeditionary Force** landed at Boulogne,

19

SIR JOHN FRENCH

43 **John French** was the overall expedition commander. Haig replaced French when French resigned in December 1915.

11 Haig believed that it was possible for the **Allies** to punch a hole in the German defences, and thus win the war, by using massive force and huge numbers of soldiers. In other words: he was ready to accept horrific losses among his own men in the belief that victory was possible by that means. The disasters of 97 120 the **Somme** and the **Third Battle of Ypres** among 62 others must be laid at his feet. **Lloyd George** never trusted him but was unable to find someone suitable to replace him. In 1919 when the war was over, Haig was still popular with the public. He was given a peerage and £100,000, a huge sum in those days. In 20 1921 he helped to form the **British Legion**, a voluntary organisation which has helped old soldiers from that time to this.

88 High Seas Fleet *see* **Scapa Flow**

Hindenburg Line
fearsome German fortification

By August 1916, it had become obvious to the German High Command that the Germans had fewer men to lose than their enemies. So as not to 63 spread German forces too thinly, **Ludendorff** decided to shorten the German lines in France by retreating several miles to make a slightly shorter front line. First, a massive system of barbed wire, trenches, deep dugouts and concrete machine gun posts was built behind the German lines. Next, in early 1917, the German army began to pull back behind this new 'Hindenburg Line'. As they pulled back they laid waste to the land they had occupied. Villages and towns were sacked, roads mined, buildings booby-trapped, wells spoiled with horse manure. Even the local people were carted off to work for the Germans in Germany or Belgium.

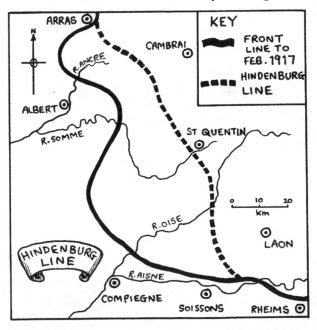

Ludendorff's plan was to fight a defensive war. He wanted the **Allies** to wear themselves out by trying to break through the Hindenburg Line. It was so strong that it was only pierced by the Allies towards the end of the war. After it fell the Germans had nothing left to defend themselves with, and the war was as good as over. **Armistice** followed soon after.

Hindenburg, Field Marshal 🧢 Paul von

very important German general

1847-1934

Generalfeldmarschall Paul Ludwig von Beneckendorf und von Hindenburg was a vain man who liked having his portrait painted, usually wearing a fancy uniform with lots of buttons and gold braid. He used to say: 'a coat without a button is like a flower without a scent'. His main talent was for looking important and being calm. That seems to have been enough. With his deputy **Erich von Ludendorff** he dominated Germany from 1916 until the end of World War I.

63

HINDENBURG

When the war started, Hindenburg had been retired from the army since 1911. He was recalled to command Germany's defences against Russia, in Prussia in the north-east. Shortly after he arrived he had the good luck to win a massive victory over the Russians at the **Battle of Tannenberg** (August 1914). The victory was due to existing plans, but Hindenburg got all the credit. From then on he was hailed as the 'saviour of East Prussia'.

104

LUDENDORFF

After the Battle of Tannenberg, Hindenburg rose to become chief of the German 'Great General Staff', replacing **Falkenhayn** during the battle of **Verdun**. He soon became more popular with the German public than **Kaiser Wilhelm** himself. Hindenburg and Ludendorff ran Germany like a war machine. They took control of German industry and food production as well as the armed forces. It wasn't until the very end of the war that the two men were forced from their perch. Hindenburg bounced back in 1925, when he was elected President of the new German Republic (the Kaiser had abdicated). In 1933, it was President Hindenburg who agreed to the appointment of another right-wing politician, called Adolf Hitler, to be Germany's Chancellor.

🚫 internment camps

unpleasant places to put foreign people

When war broke out in 1914, there were many foreigners living in Britain, including a lot of Germans who worked as waiters in London restaurants. A nasty wave of anti-foreigner feeling swept across the country. 'Aliens', as foreigners were called, were treated like enemies. Many lost their jobs and their homes were attacked by angry neighbours. Almost anyone with a foreign-sounding name was in danger. **Asquith's** government was forced to pass an act ordering all aliens between the ages of seventeen and forty-five to be sent to *'internment camps'*, prisons in all but name. There they were kept locked up until the war was over.

16

🎩 Jellicoe, Admiral Sir John

careful British sailor

1859-1935

Admiral Jellicoe, the son of a sea captain, went to sea when he was only twelve. He had forty-three years experience of the navy behind him, when he was chosen to be commander-in-chief of the British

Grand Fleet in August 1914. From then on, Jellicoe's main job was to blockade Germany by keeping the German fleet penned up in its main harbour at Wilhelmshaven on the North Sea coast. To do that, he had to make sure that British ships weren't wasted on other tasks. Because of this policy he may 53 have been too careful at the **Battle of Jutland** (May 1916). Many people blamed him for failing to take risks at Jutland and for the British failure to smash the weaker German fleet. Jellicoe went on to become First Sea Lord in 1916, but was removed from office 62 by **Lloyd George** in December 1917.

✗ Jutland, Battle of
sea battle which nobody won

The Battle of Jutland, fought about sixty miles off the coast of Jutland (northern Denmark), was the only battle fought between the main British and German fleets during World War I. No one won the battle and no one lost. On one side, the British lost more ships than the Germans, but then they had more ships to lose. On the other side, the British still had control of the sea when the battle was over. The German High Seas Fleet never dared to leave its home port at Wilhelmshaven on the North Sea again.

It started on 30 May 1916 when British code breakers discovered that the German High Seas Fleet was about to leave Wilhelmshaven. On hearing the news, 52 the massive British Grand Fleet under **Admiral Jellicoe** sailed across the North Sea to challenge the Germans. The Germans had no idea that the British Fleet was after them; their plan was to destroy a small force of British battle cruisers commanded by Admiral Beatty.

At 3.35 in the afternoon of 31 May, British and German battle cruisers opened fire on each other - and the British got the worst of it. Then at 6.30 pm, the two main fleets briefly contacted. The short battle must have made an awesome sight. Massive high-explosive shells from the battleships sent columns of water pluming up to sixty metres into the air and the waves were darkened by thick clouds of smoke and debris from direct hits on the hapless victims. The British fleet had 'crossed the T' [see inset diagram] of

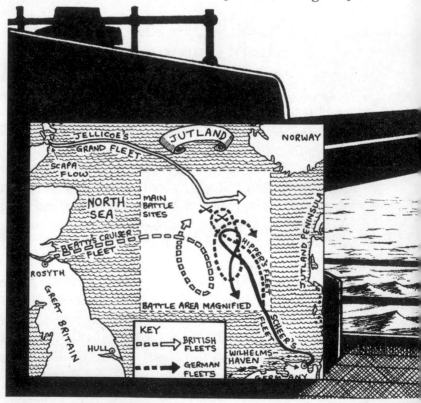

the German fleet and was far more powerful. Realising what he was up against, the German commander Admiral Scheer turned tail, a brilliant but dangerous manoeuvre. This saved most of his fleet from certain destruction. The two fleets met again at 7.10 pm when Jellicoe had another chance to destroy his enemy. He held back due to worries about torpedoes from the German destroyers.

Next morning, the Germans slipped wearily back into Wilhelmshaven - and the British stayed in control of the North Sea.

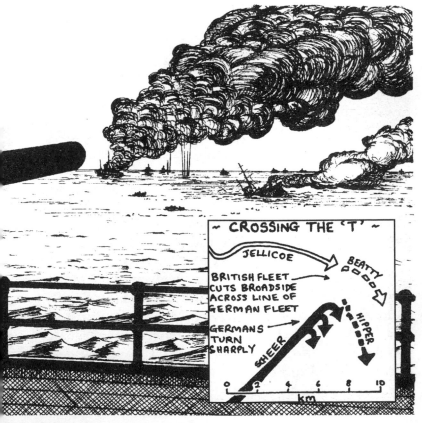

~ CROSSING THE 'T' ~

JELLICOE

BEATTY

BRITISH FLEET
CUTS BROADSIDE
ACROSS LINE OF
GERMAN FLEET

GERMANS
TURN
SHARPLY

SCHEER

HIPPER

0   2   4   6   8   10
km

 **Kaiserschlacht**

last large German offensive

By early 1918, the chessboard of World War I had changed completely from how it had been at the start of the war. In the east, Russia was out of the war because of the Russian Revolution and mutiny by Russian soldiers and sailors; in the west, America had

11 joined the **Allies** (April 1917).

50 **Hindenburg** and
63 **Ludendorff** were free to move men to France because there was no Russian army left to fight in the east - but they had to move them quickly before American forces built up.

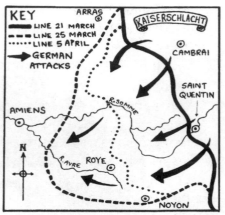

Thus *Kaiserschlacht*, means 'Kaiser's battle', the German name for their 1918 spring offensive in France. It began in heavy, early morning mist on 21 March 1918 and was aimed at a weak point in the Allied line near the town of Arras, where the French and British armies joined up. The German attack came as a complete surprise and it was brilliantly successful. By 25 March they had forced the British to fall back 40 km. Eventually however, they had to stop, due to exhaustion as much as anything else. They'd failed to break through the Allied line and they'd lost 250,000 men - men they could ill afford to lose at that stage in the war.

Kitchener armies

British volunteer armies

58 When **General Herbert Kitchener** became Secretary of State for War in August 1914, he was one of the few men in Britain who realised that the war would not be 'over by Christmas'. He understood that it would be long and bloody. At that time, all Britain had by way of an army was a small, although highly professional force - far too small for the task ahead. Many thousands, or possibly millions, of men would be needed if the Germans were to be defeated. Kitchener set out to recruit a mass, volunteer army. 54 million patriotic posters were printed with pictures of Kitchener pointing and slogans such as: 'BRITONS Join your country's army!'

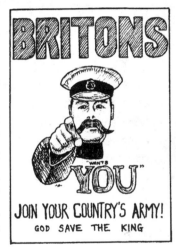

A great wave of excitement swept across the country. Men from all walks of life, from street cleaners to bank managers to lion tamers, flocked to join up. There were long queues outside recruiting offices in most town centres - the queue to join the Liverpool Scottish regiment stretched for two miles and took a week to process. Within a month, Kitchener was able to form six new divisions of volunteer regular soldiers, each of around 20,000 men, and by March 1915 he had 29 infantry divisions. With these and other divisions from the British Empire and the Territorial Force (now the Territorial Army) the total strength of Kitchener's 'new armies' was 75 divisions by mid-1915, with up to 50,000 transport animals (mainly horses but including some elephants from India).

Kitchener, Field Marshal Horatio Herbert
'Lord Kitchener of Khartoum'
war leader who built armies

1850-1916

General Kitchener was Britain's top soldier when World War I started. He had led the army which defeated the Sudanese at the famous Battle of Omdurman (1898) (the Khartoum he became lord of is the Sudanese capital). He had also commanded the British forces in the Second Boer

KITCHENER IN EGYPTIAN ARMY UNIFORM

War (1899-1902). Who better to be Secretary of State for War and to lead Britain's war effort?

Kitchener expected a long, bloody struggle and at least three million deaths. He set out to recruit a mass volunteer army. More than a million men joined up by the end of the year. The new **'Kitchener' army** gave vital strength to the old, professional **British Expeditionary Force** which was in a bad way by the end of 1914.

Kitchener was never an easy man to work with. He

57
19

had a stern, unsmiling face and he was no good at discussing things with other people. Other members of the government had to take what he said - or leave it. They weren't sorry when he set off on a mission to visit **Czar Nicholas II** of Russia in June 1916. Unfortunately, Kitchener's ship, the cruiser *Hampshire*, sank off the Orkney Islands, probably after hitting a German mine, and he was killed.

94 Kut, Siege of *see* side shows

✠ Lawrence, 🏃
Colonel T (homas) E(dward)
'Lawrence of Arabia'
clever officer who helped the Arabs
1888-1935

When World War I started, Arabia was part of the tottering Turkish Empire. The Arabs wanted independence from the Turks and, since Turkey was an ally of Germany, Britain was happy to help them. Lawrence, a British intelligence officer, became friends with Feisal Ibn Hussein, leader of the 'Arab Revolt'. Lawrence took command of a force of desert Arabs. Under his command they blew up Turkish trains and railway lines, including the main Hejaz line, which ran for 1,320 kilometres (820 miles) from Damascus to Medina (in modern Saudi Arabia). He was such a nuisance that, in 1917, the Turks offered a reward of £20,000 for the capture of 'Al Urans (Lawrence), Destroyer of Engines'.

Lawrence lived like an Arab. He spoke Arabic, wore Arab clothes and shared the hardships of his men. In 1918 he captured Damascus itself and held it for three days until the British army under
10 **General Allenby** arrived. His adventures are told in his masterpiece, *Seven Pillars of Wisdom*, first printed in 1926. A strange man, he retreated from fame when the war was over. In 1922 he enlisted in the army under a false name, as a common soldier, and later he did the same sort of thing in the RAF. He died in a motorcycle accident in Dorset after swerving to avoid two boys on bicycles.

👞 live and let live
strategies for staying alive

114 The **Western Front** stretched for five hundred miles across Belgium and northern France. Five hundred
107 miles of **trenches** which in some places were only ten to fifteen metres apart. It was quite impossible for there to be fierce fighting for four years of war all along this line. Left to themselves, most of the soldiers on both sides just wanted to stay alive. If the strangers in the other trench weren't trying to kill them, why should they try to kill the strangers? Why not 'live and let live', an expression first used in the summer of 1915.

'Cushy sectors' were the quiet patches where there was little fighting; 'active sectors' were where there was lots of it. On 'cushy sectors' the men arranged to 'let sleeping dogs lie'. The men of both sides kept an unofficial truce. There were ways of arranging it without senior officers finding out. Gunners would fire their guns at the same time and at the same place every day so that the other side could get out of the way: neither side shot at the other's toilets in case the others did the same back: no one fired during breakfast. 'Fire-eaters', men who liked fighting, were quickly put in their place. After all, if a fire-eater killed someone on the other side, the other side might fire back. The atmosphere in cushy sectors could be quite friendly. Quite a few Germans had worked in London as waiters before the war started. They spoke English so shouted conversations were possible. Some of them were interested in English football and wanted to know the scores. Men sang to the other side across **no man's land**, songs such as: *It's a long way to Tipperary* or *Deutschland über alles* and musicians were welcomed by both sides as a way to relieve the boredom.

72

Official British policy was to dominate no man's land with sniper fire and deadly night time raids, but even then the men found ways to avoid fighting. German and English patrols would pass within yards of each other without shooting, sometimes signalling with raised helmets to show that they would not fire if the other side didn't. 'Live and let live' drove the generals wild, but there was a limit to what they could do about it.

Lloyd George, David
'The New Conductor'
Prime Minister for a war

1863-1945

Lloyd George was the son of a Welsh farmer. He grew up to become one of Britain's greatest prime ministers. He was Chancellor of the Exchequer at the start of the war, but in May 1915 the Prime Minister, 16 **Herbert Asquith**, put him in charge of a new 'Munitions Ministry'. Lloyd George brought in many 117 changes and arranged for large numbers of **women** to work in Britain's armaments factories. By 1916 Britain could produce as many shells, bullets and rifles in three weeks as would have taken at least a year back in 1914.

In December 1916 Lloyd George was chosen to be Prime Minister, replacing Asquith. He was the right man for the job. As soon as he took power, he

grabbed the country by the scruff of its war-weary
33 neck and gave it a good shaking. The **convoy** system
81 was started, **rationing** was improved and more men
were recruited into the army.

Lloyd George never trusted
47 **Douglas Haig**. He always
hoped to move the focus of
the war away from the muddy
killing fields of Belgium and
France. But despite this, he
gave Haig permission to
120 launch the disastrous **Third**

Battle of Ypres, otherwise known as Passchendaele.
When it became clear that the battle was a futile
blood bath, he longed to sack Haig but was unsure
who could replace him.

Lloyd George was very popular with the British
public during the war, and in November 1918 he was
re-elected with a massive majority. He was finally
forced out in 1922 by conservative members of his
own government. He lived on, a brooding, giant
figure in the background of British life, for another
twenty-three years. He was buried in Wales, in a
quiet spot by a river where he used to play as a boy.

Ludendorff, General Erich von

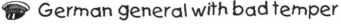 German general with bad temper

1865-1937

Erich Ludendorff was a cold fish with no sense of
humour. He always wore a monocle (single eyeglass)
and had a red face and droopy jaws, which wobbled

⁵⁰ when he lost his temper. He and **General Hindenburg** led Germany for the second half of the war. Both men rose to fame after the German victory ¹⁰⁴ at **Tannenberg** on 30 August 1914, against the Russians. Of the two of them, Ludendorff did most of the hard work.

Their rule began in 1916, when Hindenburg became commander of the 'Great German Army'. Beside him, as 'First Quartermaster General' (a title which he made up himself), Ludendorff pulled the strings which actually ran the country. He was extremely ⁹⁹ warlike, ordering the start of total **submarine** warfare against British and American ships in 1917, which led to America joining the war and proved to be a bad mistake for the Germans. Almost to the end, Ludendorff believed in victory at all costs. In August 1918, after it became obvious that victory at *any* cost

was impossible, he had a nervous breakdown. He took to drink and crying suddenly for no reason. He was told to rest, to sing German folk songs on waking - and stop talking in a 'high shrill voice of command'. On 26 October 1918 he resigned, to the great relief of the German people. Later he campaigned against Jews, Jesuits* and Freemasons and sat for two years as a Nazi member of the German parliament.

Lusitania
British liner sunk by a submarine

On 7 May 1915, the British luxury liner *Lusitania* was steaming home from New York to Liverpool. She was on the last leg of her journey and had rounded the southern tip of Ireland. On board were more than 1,900 passengers and crew. Also on board was a cargo of 173 tons of small arms and ammunition for the British army in France. The Germans knew about the arms and ammunition. They had advertised in the New York newspapers, warning people not to sail on the liner because they intended to attack her if they could.

99 The German **submarine** U-20, commanded by Captain Walter Schweiger, was cruising in the Irish Sea off the port of Kinsale when the *Lusitania* steamed into the Irish Sea, directly into his path. His instructions were clear. One torpedo slammed into the great ship amidships. It exploded causing another, larger explosion, probably in the ship's boilers. In just eighteen minutes the *Lusitania* had disappeared beneath the waves. 1,198 people died, 94 of them children.

128 American citizens were among the dead. This caused outrage in America, where public opinion began to turn against Germany. This prepared the ground for when America eventually entered the war in April 1917.

⚔ machine guns
weapon which ruled the trenches

World War I is known as the 'machine gun war'. It was because of machine guns more than anything else that attack became so difficult and defence so easy. The defenders had their trenches for protection but, once they left their own trenches, the attackers had nothing to protect them. A single machine gun, firing 400-600 rounds per minute, could cut down a line of soldiers in less than a minute - and usually it 72 took more than a minute to cross **no man's land**.

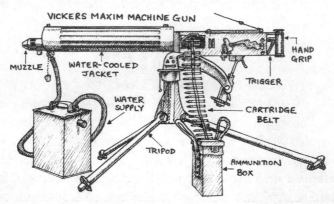

VICKERS MAXIM MACHINE GUN

MUZZLE

WATER-COOLED JACKET

WATER SUPPLY

HAND GRIP

TRIGGER

CARTRIDGE BELT

TRIPOD

AMMUNITION BOX

Because they fired their bullets so quickly, machine gun barrels tended to overheat and the guns jammed. Barrels were cooled either from water bags, with a sort of jacket of water wrapped around the barrel, or by air vents. The guns were usually positioned in groups of three so that even if two of them jammed there was still one left to keep firing. At the start of the war, there were only heavy machine guns, such as the British Vickers gun which was mounted on a tripod for firing and could weigh up to 60 kg. Weapons such as this needed crews of six men to carry and fire them. However, lighter models were soon developed, such as the Lewis gun, weighing around 14 kg. Light machine guns could be carried by one man and were mostly air cooled, and because they were easier to carry they could be used for attack as well as defence. They were also mounted on aeroplanes.

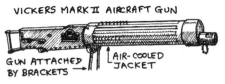

VICKERS MARK II AIRCRAFT GUN

GUN ATTACHED BY BRACKETS →

AIR-COOLED JACKET

✗ Marne, First Battle of the
battle which saved Paris

On 4 August 1914, at the beginning of the war, the Germans invaded France through Belgium. They swept all before them and within a month German armies were only 60 km from Paris. It looked as though the city would fall within days. The French government left for Bordeaux on 2 September and up to 500,000 French civilians also left the city.

19   However, although the French armies and the **BEF** had fallen back before the Germans, they'd not been completely smashed. They had a lucky break when General von Kluck, commander of the German 1st army, decided to change direction in order to encircle Paris from the east rather than the west. This meant that one flank of von Kluck's army was now facing the French. On 6 September, the French 6th army attacked. Other French armies also stopped retreating. They re-crossed the river Marne and flung themselves against the Germans. The BEF poured through a gap which opened between the German 1st and 2nd armies. The immense battle

raged back and forth from 6th-12th of September, involving more than two million men. At one point the French 6th army nearly collapsed and had to be reinforced by 6,000 soldiers from Paris who were driven to the front in 600 taxis. Finally the Germans were forced to retreat. They dug in along the river Aisne to the north.

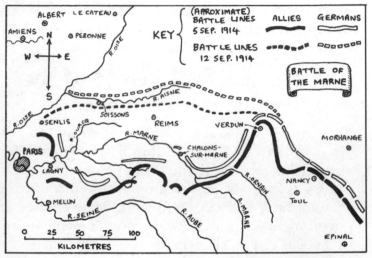

And there they stayed, with a few minor changes -
107 for the next four years of **trench** warfare. According
89 to the **Schlieffen Plan**, Germany had needed a quick victory in the west so as to free German troops for victory over the Russians to the east. Because of the Battle of the Marne, German troops were stuck in France, and Germany would have to fight in the east and the west at the same time. In a sense, the Battle of the Marne was when the Germans lost the war - and it happened just a month after the war started.

94 Mesopotamia *see* **side shows**

120 Messines Ridge *see* **Ypres, Third Battle of**

⤙ Mills bombs
easy-throwing grenades

107 Hand grenades were very useful in **trench** warfare for destroying or stunning all the soldiers in an enemy trench. The blast from the grenade was channelled down the trench. The *Mills bomb* was a British hand grenade which could be thrown about twenty-five metres. The cast iron case was specially weakened in places so that it burst into fragments of shrapnel when the bomb exploded. 33 million Mills bombs were issued during the course of the war. At the height of the fighting in 1916, the
19 **BEF** was throwing 800,000 of them per week.

✗ Mons, Battle of
first German v. British battle

19 On 23 August 1914, the **BEF**, having just arrived on the continent, was moving cautiously inland from the Belgian coast and had almost reached the Mons canal, near the border with France, when they came up against the German 1st army. It was the first time in the war that Germans and British met in battle. The Germans had 160,000 soldiers with 600 heavy guns; the British had 70,000 soldiers and just 300 heavy guns. Despite the unequal size of the two
83 armies, expert British **rifle** fire caused terrible losses.
43 Eventually however, the British commander **Field Marshal French** realised how outnumbered he was and the British retreated. Their retreat ended a
67 month later outside Paris, at the **Battle of the Marne**.

mortars
big gun, short barrel

A mortar is a gun with a very short, wide barrel which lobs its shell in a high curve so that it falls sharply to earth. Mortars were first developed in the late Middle Ages and were used for firing over the top of castle and city walls. They went rather out of fashion for several hundred years but came into their own again in World War I, when they were very useful in **trench** warfare.

107

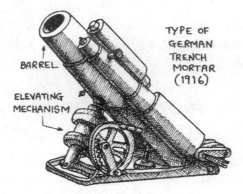

BARREL

ELEVATING
MECHANISM

TYPE OF
GERMAN
TRENCH
MORTAR
(1916)

Mortars are designed to fire the heaviest possible shell over a short distance. The largest British mortar shell, the 'flying pig', 68 kg of high explosive and not far off 1.5 metres long, only travelled about 1000 metres. The Germans had an even bigger one of 90 kg which travelled only 600 metres. Because their shells only travelled short distances, mortars had to be light enough to be carried near to the enemy trenches. Mortar crews were made up of strong and extremely brave men - mortar 'suicide clubs' were usually made up of the toughest men in a battalion.

👑 Nicholas II, Czar
emperor who lost his empire
1868-1919

Nicholas II was the supreme ruler of the Russian Empire, appointed by God or so he believed. If the truth be told, he wasn't very clever, and he was frightened of his best ministers because he knew that they were cleverer than he was. After war broke out, he became very unpopular, even among his troops. Russian soldiers were poorly-supplied and poorly-led and Russian armies kept losing to the Germans. In February 1917, there was a public uprising against Nicholas's government in St. Petersburg, then the Russian capital. Several regiments mutinied and refused to stop the uprising. Power slipped from his fingers and on 15 March he was forced to abdicate*. He would have liked to flee to England, but England didn't want him and neither did France. On the night of 16/17 July 1919, he and his family were shot in cold blood in the cellar of the house where they were imprisoned in Yekaterinburg, on orders from the new **Bolshevik** government.

19

YEKATERINBURG
ⓞ

72 **Nivelle Offensive** *see* **Nivelle, General Robert**

🎩 Nivelle, General Robert
offensive French general
1856-1924

111 General Nivelle first rose to fame as commander of the French defences at **Verdun** early in 1916. That December, he replaced Joffre as Commander-in-Chief of all the French armies. Nivelle believed that the Germans were weakening and that the Allies could end the war quickly if they attacked hard 62 enough. **Lloyd George** believed him and placed the 19 **BEF** under his command. On April 1917 Nivelle launched a massive attack on German positions. But the 'Nivelle offensive' was a disaster. Huge numbers of French soldiers were killed for very small gains. Sections of the French army mutinied in the following month and on 15 May Nivelle lost his job to 75 **General Pétain**.

👞 no man's land
between the trenches

In early English, *nomannesland* meant an area of land where ownership was unclear. By the Middle Ages it had become the name for a strip of land outside the north walls of the City of London where criminals were executed. In World War I, it came to mean the strip of dead ground between German and Allied 107 **trenches**, a ghastly wasteland, cratered by shell holes, where dead bodies rotted away because it was too dangerous to remove them. At night raiding parties ventured out to probe enemy defences but in the day it was deserted. No man's land ran for five hundred miles, the length of the front in western Europe. In some places it was almost a kilometre wide, in others it shrank to as little as twenty metres or less.

Old Contemptibles
brave British soldiers

19 In 1914 at the start of the war, the **British Expeditionary Force** which crossed the Channel to Belgium was small, just one cavalry division and four 115 infantry divisions. **Kaiser Wilhelm** called them a 'contemptible little army' because there were so few of them. From that time on, the soldiers of that first force to cross the Channel, the men who fought at 69 the **Battle of Mons**, who were actually very professional, wore the name 'Old Contemptibles' with pride.

Owen, Wilfrid
war poet and soldier
1893-1918

Above all I am not concerned with Poetry. My subject is War, and the pity of War. The Poetry is in the pity.

Wilfrid Owen, the son of a railway clerk, was brought up in the quiet county town of Shrewsbury. He enlisted in the army on 14 September 1915. The difference between the gentle world of his childhood and the horror of the trenches was truly shocking. Unlike **Rupert Brooke**, Owen never thought that war could be beautiful or exciting. It was horrific from the start. In one of the first poems which he wrote in the trenches, *At a Calvary near Ancre*, he compares the suffering of Christ on the cross with the suffering of soldiers.

In May 1917 he was sent to Craiglockhart Hospital in Scotland, suffering from neurasthenia, a type of mental disorder. There he met **Siegfried Sassoon**, also a patient. It was the most important meeting of Owen's life. His later poems such as *Anthem for Doomed Youth* are influenced by Sassoon's criticisms.

Owen returned to the front in September 1918 and fought bravely. He was killed while crossing the Sambre and Oise canal in the early morning of 4 November 1918, a week before the **Armistice**.

Palestine *see* **Allenby, General** and **side shows**.

🏃 pals' battalions
they joined up together

In the surge of excitement at the start of the war, men joined the army in tens of thousands. Some of them joined up in groups and were formed into *'pals' battalions'*, made up of men who knew each other in civilian* life. They might be old boys from the same school such as the 'Grimsby Chums' from Wintringham school in Grimsby, or they might belong to the same sports club, or just come from the same town or industry. Men from all classes joined them, from chimney sweeps to 'nuts' (pre-war, upper class dandies).

The problem with pals' battalions was that, given the conditions of warfare on the western front, they might all be wiped out in a single attack. If that happened, a town or city could lose nearly all its young men in one go - which is exactly what did 97 happen to several communities during the **Battle of the Somme** in July 1916, when the loss of British life was truly appalling. After the Somme, it was generally felt that pals' battalions were a bad idea and that it was better to spread the losses more evenly around the country.

120 Passchendaele *see* **Ypres, Third Battle of**

Pétain, General Henri Philipe
French hero - and French traitor

1856-1951

Philipe Pétain was asked to command the French 111 defence of **Verdun** on 26 February 1916. There he inspired his men to acts of incredible heroism. Due to this success, on 15 May 1917, he was made Commander-in-Chief of the French armies (after the ⁷² mutinies caused by **Nivelle's** disastrous offensive). He improved conditions for the troops and restored order with a minimum of force.

In 1940 after Hitler invaded France at the start of World War II, Pétain came out of retirement to head the Vichy government of the part of southern France unoccupied by the Germans, called after its capital, the small town of Vichy. Pétain was eighty-three and he believed that France's only hope was to cooperate with her conquerors. After the war he was tried as a traitor and sentenced to death, but this sentence was reduced to solitary confinement for life.

planes
a new way of fighting

Heavier-than-air, powered flight was only eleven years old when World War I broke out. The Allies and their German enemies had less than two hundred planes between them. By the end of the war, thousands of planes were in action on both sides, and German bombers were raiding as far as England.

To start with, planes were used for reconnaissance - to gather information on enemy positions and to ¹⁴ help the **artillery** to target their guns. There was no radio, which was still pretty useless even at the end of the war, so the pilots communicated with the ground by landing or by dropping messages. Ground control communicated back by means of 'panels', strips of black and white cloth laid out in the fields. The patterns were a code: different layouts meant different, simple messages.

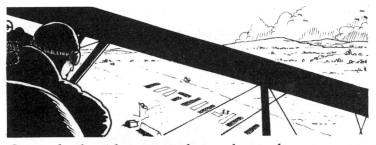

Soon, both sides started to shoot down enemy reconnaissance planes and so they started to arm their planes. Confused 'dogfights' developed, sometimes of up to a hundred planes all diving and weaving in the sky over the trenches. Tactics were basically the same then as now: surprise attacks are best, get behind your opponent and fly with the sun behind you to blind him. Up in the air, planes communicated with each other by tipping their wings or with hand signals. Skilled pilots were known as 'aces'. **Manfred von Richthofen**, Germany's most famous ace, notched up eighty kills before he was shot down in April 1918.

A COMMEMORATIVE POSTCARD (c. 1917)

The average speed of the planes was around 160 kph (100 mph) and the light machine guns which they carried had an accurate range of less than 200 metres, so air fighting was close up and extremely dangerous. During 'Bloody April' in 1917, British pilots could expect to live an average of just twenty-three days after they arrived at the front. Parachutes were primitive and pilots weren't allowed them anyway (except German pilots towards the end of the war) in case they bailed out early to avoid danger. 50,000 airmen died before the war was over.

Despite the danger, war in the air was always more gentlemanly than war on the ground. Pilots would stop firing once an enemy plane was obviously out of action. They might even fly over and drop a wreath at the spot where they'd shot someone down. And pilots who had to land in enemy territory were usually well treated. Many flew with a toothbrush and other simple comforts ready packed in case this happened, although the higher-ups disapproved of this as they did of parachutes, in case pilots gave up too easily.

Most World War I planes were biplanes (two sets of wings one above the other), although there were also triplanes (three wings). The most famous British planes were the *Sopwith Camel* (named after the hump on the body where the machine gun was placed) and the *Sopwith Pup*. The best French plane was the *Spad* and the Germans had *Fokkers*, *Albatrosses*, and *Gothas*, the heavy twin-engined, long

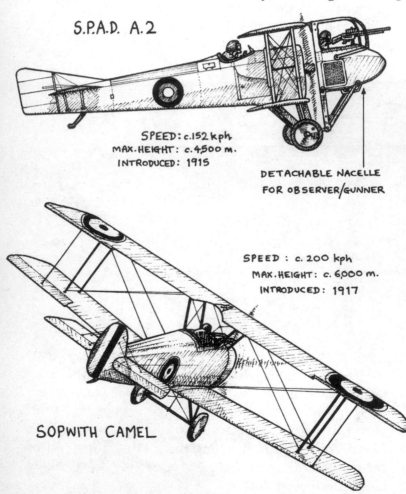

S.P.A.D. A.2

SPEED: c.152 kph
MAX.HEIGHT: c.4,500 m.
INTRODUCED: 1915

DETACHABLE NACELLE
FOR OBSERVER/GUNNER

SPEED : c. 200 kph
MAX.HEIGHT: c. 6,000 m.
INTRODUCED: 1917

SOPWITH CAMEL

distance bombers which were used to bomb London. On the whole the Germans kept a step ahead with new technology throughout the war. It was the Germans who employed Dutchman Anthony Fokker after the Allies had turned him down. Fokker invented the 'gear', where the speed of fire of the machine gun was timed so that it fired through the propeller without hitting the blades.

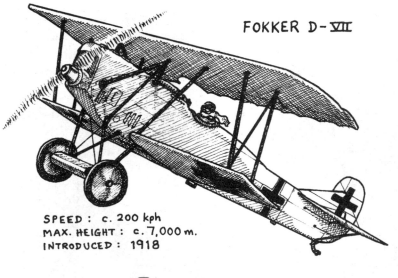

FOKKER D-VII

SPEED : c. 200 kph
MAX. HEIGHT : c. 7,000 m.
INTRODUCED : 1918

 rationing
sharing out scraps

War disrupted food supplies in many ways. Two thirds of Britain's sugar had been produced from German sugar beet before the war. Once war started, Britain went short of sugar - countries at war with each other are hardly going to sell each other sugar. Meanwhile, German **submarines** sank British ships carrying food from overseas and the Royal Navy blockaded Germany.

99

In Britain, shortages led to queues for basic foods. Thousands might queue outside a single shop - in Walworth Road, London in 1916, around 3,000 people queued for margarine. Things got better after December 1916, when **Lloyd George**, the 'New Conductor' as he was called, became Prime Minister. Lloyd George's regulations were tough but they were fair. Quite small things were forbidden: to throw rice at weddings, to feed scraps to pets, even to starch your collar. It was Lloyd George who introduced rationing and that was tough too, so tough that if you stuck to the official rations you probably felt hungry! But at least, once rations were introduced, food was handed out more fairly between rich and poor. In fact, working class people probably ate better during the war than before it broke out, when often all they could afford to eat was bread.

In Germany food shortages were far more severe, mainly due to the British blockade. Three quarters of a million Germans died of starvation.

12 Remembrance Day *see* **Armistice**

✠ Richthofen, Manfred von
'The Red Baron'
top German flying ace
1892-1918

Manfred von Richthofen joined the German Army Air Service in May 1915, becoming the most successful fighter 'ace' of either side during the war. He shot down a total of eighty enemy **planes**. His squad was known as 'Richthofen's Flying Circus' and he himself was called the 'Red Baron' because the planes were painted scarlet. When he was shot down on 21 April 1918, his body was laid out in a British hangar and hundreds of British soldiers and airmen filed past to pay their respects.

76

⚞ rifles
the aim of it all

Rifles were the basic infantry weapon of World War I. Mostly they were repeating rifles and could fire from five to ten rounds before they had to be reloaded. Up-to-date models, such as British Lee Enfields and German Mausers were accurate to over 600 metres and roughly accurate up to 1,400 metres. Expert marksmen were used as snipers by both sides to pick off any enemy soldier unwise enough to show his head above the parapet of his **trench**.

107

Rifles were often fired in devastating volleys. Speed of fire was essential, especially to stop attackers before they could reach you. After all, one soldier firing ten rounds per minute is worth two soldiers firing five rounds per minute. At the **Battle of Mons** in August 1914, the professional British soldiers made up for their lack of numbers by their speed of fire. They could average fifteen rounds per minute.

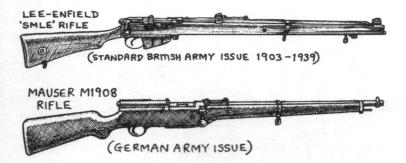

LEE-ENFIELD 'SMLE' RIFLE

(STANDARD BRITISH ARMY ISSUE 1903–1939)

MAUSER M1908 RIFLE

(GERMAN ARMY ISSUE)

Soldiers in all armies were given bayonets for close-up fighting. They were attached to the barrel of a rifle to turn it into a stabbing weapon. In actual fact, most experienced soldiers preferred home-made clubs, daggers and knuckledusters to bayonets when it came to hand-to-hand fighting.

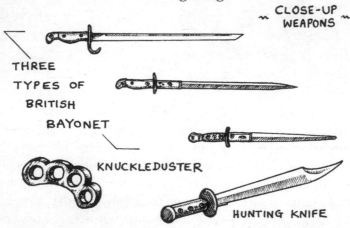

~ CLOSE-UP WEAPONS ~

THREE TYPES OF BRITISH BAYONET

KNUCKLEDUSTER

HUNTING KNIFE

94 Romania *see* **side shows**

19 Russian Revolution *see* **Bolsheviks**

Salonika
up a Greek creek
(*see also* side shows)

27 In October 1915, Serbia was under threat of invasion by the **Central Powers**. Bulgaria had joined the war on the German side on 11 October so Serbia was under threat from Bulgarians in the east as well as Austrians in the north. Serbia desperately needed help from the Allies.

The best way to transport French and British troops was via Salonika, a Greek port on the Aegean Sea.

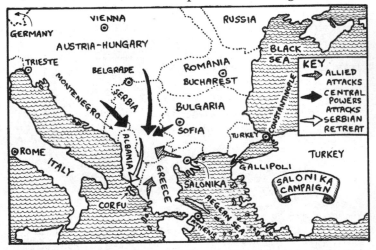

43 From there, there was a railway line to Belgrade, the Serbian capital. The first French and British troops duly landed in Salonika from **Gallipoli** on 15 October 1915. Meanwhile, the Central Powers

invaded Serbia and the small Serbian army was forced to retreat. The Serbian king and government army left their country in a dangerous and heroic march, the 'Great Retreat', through the mountains of Albania. The Serbs were then taken from the Albanian coast to the island of Corfu by ships of the Royal Navy. Meanwhile, the **Allies** attempting to help them from Salonika were forced back into the area surrounding the town.

For the rest of the war, apart from a few futile attempts to break out, the Allied 'Army of the East' was stuck in Salonika. By early 1917 it had swollen to nearly a million men, made up of French and British reinforcements, the Serbian army now shipped from Corfu and a small force of Russians. They dug themselves in behind a network of **trenches** and other fortifications. It wasn't until September 1918 that they finally drove the Central Powers out of Serbia.

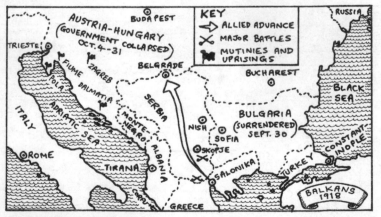

The Allies lost 20,000 men in battle during the Salonika campaign, not much by World War I standards. However, due to the humid and unhealthy conditions, 450,000 men caught malaria and most of the men spent time in hospital.

✠ 🏃 Sassoon, Siegfried ✒
'Mad Jack'
poet and hero
1886-1967

Siegfried Sassoon lived the life of a carefree young gentleman until war broke out in 1914, hunting, visiting friends and writing rather ordinary poems. In 1915, he enlisted as an officer in the Royal Welsh Fusiliers and turned out to be a brave soldier. His friends called him 'Mad Jack'. He once captured a German trench single-handed.

War turned Mad Jack into a great poet. His poems are full of anger at the suffering of the soldiers and the stupidity of senior officers. In April 1917 he was wounded, and while recovering he wrote a letter which was read out in the House of Commons:

I am making this statement as an act of wilful defiance of military authority because I believe that the war is being deliberately prolonged by those who have the power to end it ...

Such a statement by a war hero was very embarrassing for the top brass of the army. Sassoon was declared to be suffering from **shell shock** and was sent to the War Hospital at Craiglockhart in Scotland, where he met his fellow war poet **Wilfrid Owen**. The following year he was judged fit to fight again, but in July he was wounded for the second time, this time in the head. Invalided out, the war was over for him. He lived on for many years. In 1928 he published *Memoirs of a Fox-Hunting Man*, an elegy for the carefree life he had lived before war began.

Scapa Flow
safe haven for ships off Scotland

Scapa Flow is a safe anchorage for large ships among the Orkney islands off the north coast of Scotland. For most of World War I it was the main base of the Royal Navy, although at the beginning of the war the navy was forced to anchor off northern Ireland due to lack of defences against German **submarines**. Scapa Flow was also used as a naval base in World War II. It was finally closed in 1956.

After the **Armistice** at the end of World War I, the German High Seas Fleet steamed to Scotland and surrendered in Scottish waters (21 November 1918). All the best German ships were then taken to Scapa Flow. On 21 June 1919, the Germans scuttled their ships and sent them to the bottom rather than leave them any longer in the hands of the British.

Schlieffen Plan
German plan that backfired

Long before World War I, German planners knew that Germany might have to fight France in the west and Russia in the east at the same time - France and Russia became allies in 1892. General Alfred Graf von Schlieffen, Chief of the 'Great General Staff' of the German army 1891-1904, thought up a plan to defeat France first and then finish off Russia afterwards.

Schlieffen calculated that, Russia being so huge and backward, it would take the Russian army at least six weeks to get ready after war was declared. So Germany would have six short weeks in which to defeat France. The border between France and Germany was defended by a line of French forts, forts which would slow down the German armies. To beat the French within six weeks, the Germans must attack from the west in a swooping curve through neutral Belgium.

By attacking from the west they would avoid the French forts. They would also hit the French in the flank and cut off the French line of retreat to the south. After defeating France, the Germans could then move most of their troops to the east and defeat Russia. That was the *Schlieffen Plan*.

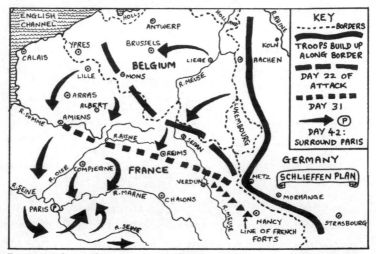

It went horribly wrong almost as soon as World War I started. The Germans swept through Belgium as planned, but then, at the **Battle of the Marne**, the main German attack was stopped in its tracks outside Paris by the French and their British allies. Meanwhile the Russians had entered the war so the Germans had to fight in the east and the west at the same time - exactly what they'd hoped to avoid.

shell shock

the madness of war

War is horrific. Soldiers have to put up with more suffering, hardship, danger and sadness than human beings were designed to cope with. Often their training sees them through but some of them get shell shock, sometimes called 'battle fatigue', or nowadays a type of 'post-traumatic stress syndrome', from the stress of it all. World War I was especially horrific and many soldiers got shell shock.

The symptoms of shell shock are: extreme sensitivity to sudden noises and bright light, sudden jerking or jumping as if surprised, disturbed sleep and nightmares of battle, and irritability which can lead to violence.

 ships

battleships to torpedo boats - and things in between

In 1914, Britain had the largest fleet of warships in the world. It was reckoned by British naval planners that the Royal Navy had to be as powerful as the two next most powerful navies put together in order to protect the vast British Empire. This was the age of the big battleship. Modelled on the revolutionary British *Dreadnought* of 1906, these floating fortresses ruled the world's oceans. Dreadnoughts could fire their massive shells accurately up to 20 kilometres and cruised at around 20 knots*. They were immense. *Dreadnought* itself had a crew of 862 men and others had crews of about the same size. Britain had 22 dreadnoughts and 29 slightly earlier battleships; Germany had 37 battleships in total.

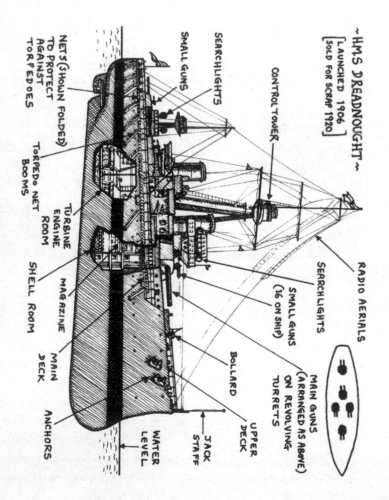

~ HMS DREADNOUGHT ~
[LAUNCHED 1906
SOLD FOR SCRAP 1920]

CONTROL TOWER

SEARCHLIGHTS

SMALL GUNS

NETS (SHOWN FOLDED)
TO PROTECT
AGAINST
TORPEDOES

TORPEDO NET
BOOMS

TURBINE
ENGINE
ROOM

MAGAZINE

SHELL ROOM

MAIN DECK

ANCHORS

WATER LEVEL

JACK STAFF

UPPER DECK

BOLLARD

SMALL GUNS
(16 ON SHIP)

SEARCHLIGHTS

RADIO AERIALS

MAIN GUNS
(ARRANGED AS ABOVE)
ON REVOLVING
TURRETS

After battleships, the next largest ships were cruisers. These had guns as powerful as battleships but were lighter and faster because they had less steel armour to protect them. Lack of armour made them
53 vulnerable. At the **Battle of Jutland** the British cruiser *Invincible* was smashed by a single shot. Britain had 10 battle cruisers, 35 cruisers and 150 older cruisers which were a bit out of date. Germany had far fewer.

~COMPARATIVE SIZES OF WARSHIPS~

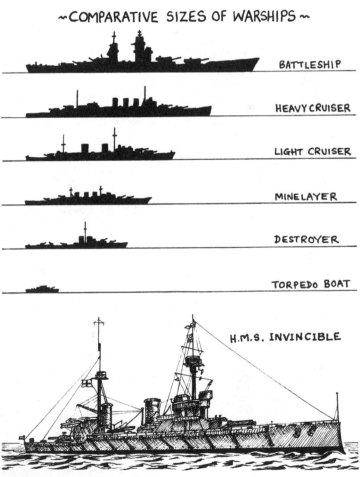

BATTLESHIP

HEAVY CRUISER

LIGHT CRUISER

MINELAYER

DESTROYER

TORPEDO BOAT

H.M.S. INVINCIBLE

By 1914, torpedoes, first developed in the 1860s, had become quite accurate. A single torpedo, launched either from a submarine, a small, fast torpedo boat or a destroyer, could sink the largest battleship if it hit in the right place. So battleships, which made a big target, never sailed without a 'screen' of small, fast destroyers to protect them. Britain had more than 200 destroyers.

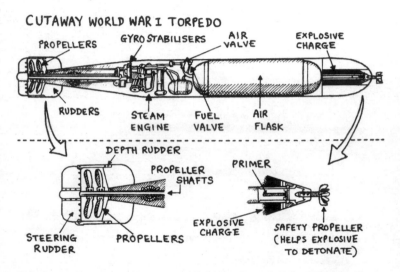

CUTAWAY WORLD WAR I TORPEDO

During the war, the Royal Navy lost 2 dreadnoughts, 11 pre-dreadnoughts, 28 cruisers, 64 destroyers, 54 submarines, 10 torpedo boats - and 34,642 men.

 **side shows**
what happened elsewhere

The main battlegrounds of World War I were on the Western Front in France and in the east between Germany and Russia. 'Side show' was the British name for other conflicts away from the main action.

There were side shows in Africa, the Balkans, the Far
43 East, **Gallipoli**, Mesopotamia, Palestine and Romania.

AFRICA was really a side
show among side
shows. The war was
mainly fought by small
troops of African
soldiers commanded by
German or British
officers. Fighting was
for control of the
European countries'
African colonies.
Perhaps the most
colourful episode of the

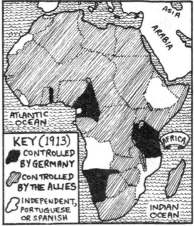

African war was a British expedition to capture Lake
Tanganyika. Led by eccentric commander Spicer
Samson, two gun boats were dragged to the lake by
rail and overland. On arrival, Spicer wore a woman's
skirt and showed off his tattoos to impress the locals.
The British won the lake.

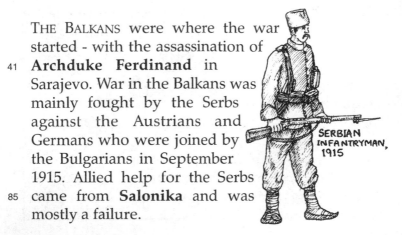

THE BALKANS were where the war
started - with the assassination of
41 **Archduke Ferdinand** in
Sarajevo. War in the Balkans was
mainly fought by the Serbs
against the Austrians and
Germans who were joined by
the Bulgarians in September
1915. Allied help for the Serbs
85 came from **Salonika** and was
mostly a failure.

SERBIAN
INFANTRYMAN,
1915

95

IN THE FAR EAST, Japan declared war on Germany in August 1914 and immediately seized German-held islands in the Pacific. Japan went on to invade China, the excuse being that there was a German colony there.

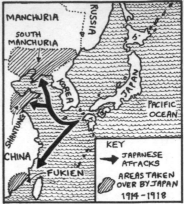

43
29 **Gallipoli** was a failure. It lost **Winston Churchill** his job as First Sea Lord and cost 140,000 British dead.

IN SOUTHERN MESOPOTAMIA, British forces seized control of part of what is now modern Iraq to protect British-controlled oil supplies from capture by the Turks. From there an Anglo-Indian force, sent from British India, advanced on Baghdad, to the north. They were forced back to the small town of Kut on 7 December 1915. The Seige of Kut was a disgrace for the British. Their force was starved into submission by the Turks and had to surrender on 30 April 1916. From then on, Anglo-Indian forces in Mesopotamia were gradually reinforced so that by the end of the war 250,000 Anglo-Indian troops faced only 50,000 badly equipped Turks. Baghdad was taken on 11 March 1917

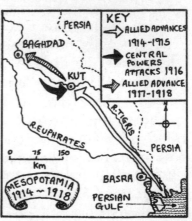

and the rest of Mesopotamia followed. This side show cost 97,579 Anglo-Indian casualties and probably more than that on the Turkish side.

PALESTINE was the main setting for the British campaign against the Turks in the Middle East. The British forces were successfully led by **General Allenby**. The British lost 51,451 dead and wounded.

ROMANIA declared war on Germany in August 1916, thus joining the **Allies**. By December Germany had conquered the richest Romanian provinces including the Romanian oilfields. The Germans took all the food and fuel they could lay their hands on. About 500,000 Romanian civilians died because of the German occupation.

⚔ Somme, First Battle of
horrific battle in northern France

The First Battle of the Somme (the Second was a German attack in 1918) began on 23 June 1916, when British artillery opened fire on German positions along the River Somme in north-west France. The barrage was so loud that the rumble of the guns could be heard across the English Channel in southern England. Over the next eight days 1.5

million shells were fired. Even the rats in the German trenches panicked and took shelter in the dugouts of the German soldiers.

The dugouts, up to nine metres deep in the chalky ground, were too deep to be damaged. When, at 7.30 am on 1 July, the British infantry attacked, the Germans were ready for them. 750,000 British soldiers went 'over the top' that day - into a blizzard

66
83

of **machine gun** and **rifle fire**. The sound of the bullets was said to have been like the 'humming of hosts of bees'. Due to the artillery barrage there was no element of surprise. The British suffered 60,000 casualties on the first day of the battle.

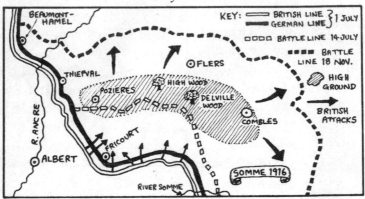

The Somme attack was meant to draw the Germans away from their own terrible attack on the French at

111

Verdun, where the French were almost on their knees, and to that extent it succeeded - a little. When the battle ended, in a snowstorm on 18 November 1916, casualties ran at around 650,000 Germans, 195,000 Frenchmen and 420,000 British. For that loss

11

the **Allies** had gained approximately five kilometres of ground. It was after the Battle of the Somme that British people started to grow weary of the war. In

Britain anxious crowds became a common sight. They gathered to read the lists of dead pasted daily in the windows of newsagents and to greet the eternal hospital trains from France. The Somme also ⁷⁴ meant the end of the **Pals' Battalions**. Too many towns had lost all their young men in one go.

 ## submarines

a mouldy way to travel

Submarines, also known as 'tinfish', 'kippers' or 'mouldies' by the sailors of the Royal Navy, were first used successfully in the American Civil War in the 1860s. Technical developments, in particular the development of torpedoes, meant that by the start of World War I submarines had become a very dangerous weapon. This was proved near the start of the war: on the morning of 22 September 1914, a German submarine torpedoed three British battle cruisers, HMSs *Hogue*, *Cressy* and *Aboukir*, in less than an hour before breakfast. 1,459 British sailors died as the three cruisers went down. Naval warfare was never the same again.

GERMAN NEWSPAPER HEADLINE:
'IN ONE DAY!'

an einem Tag!

SUNK BY U9 SUBMARINE: COMMANDED BY LT. OTTO WEDDIGEN

The average submarine of 1914-18 was about 60 metres long and could dive to a depth of up to 60 metres. Mostly they used diesel engines for surface travel and all of them used battery-powered electric motors underwater. Diesel of course won't burn without air to burn in. They could travel long distances without refuelling. German U-boats (stands for *Unterseeboot* meaning 'under-sea-ship') could travel up to 6,500 km on the surface and for 130 km under water.

Submarines were hideously uncomfortable. There were no toilets on the earliest ships. Even on later ones, many men took drugs to stop them having to use the toilets, which became absolutely disgusting on a long voyage. The smell of diesel fumes, unwashed bodies and reeking toilets was enough to turn the strongest stomach - if it wasn't already turned by the tossing and rolling of the long, thin hull. Because the air in U-boats was always a lot warmer than the surrounding water, this led to condensation on the steel plating. The condensation dripped onto sleepers' faces if they didn't cover themselves with something waterproof when they lay in their bunks.

Conditions were cramped. On some U-boats the warrant officer's bunk was so narrow that he had to lie on his side and couldn't turn over. On British submarines 'hot bunking' was normal: two men shared the same bunk, taking it in turns to sleep. In fact, on a standard E-type British submarine, it was only the captain who had a regular bunk at all. In addition to discomfort, there was also danger. Not just the danger of being shot at by the enemy but also the danger of getting drunk on diesel fumes. Crews kept mice on board. The mice's sensitive noses detected diesel fumes early and their squeaking alerted the crew.

During the war, the Germans lost 192 U-boats sunk and 5,400 killed. The British lost 54 submarines and about 1,600 killed.

WIE GEHTS, LOTTIE?

⊘ suffragettes ♀
women on the warpath

British suffragettes had fought for women's right to vote for more than ten years before World War I started. The British authorities had tried hard to stop them, ending their hunger strikes by brutal force-feeding, sending them to prison and letting them out again under the 'cat and mouse' act of 1913. All that changed when the war started. The government needed the help of **women** if Britain was to win. If the suffragettes would encourage women to work in the armament factories and on the land and as volunteers, it was generally understood that in return women would be granted the vote after the war was over. This policy was approved by Parliament in 1916.

117

Sure enough, in 1918, women over the age of thirty were granted the right to vote and in 1928 this was extended to all women over the age of twenty-one - the same as men at that time.

tanks

armour-plated monsters on tracks

For most of World War I, defenders held nearly all the cards. They could hide in their trenches, safe from enemy fire, then pop up and mow down the attackers when the time came. Once they left their own trenches, the attackers had no protection from the fire of the defenders unless they could capture the enemy trench and shelter in it. Tanks changed all that.

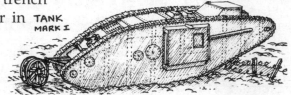

TANK MARK I

29 **Winston Churchill**, as First Sea Lord, was the first British minister to understand how important tanks would be. That's why the earliest tanks were developed by a 'Landships Committee' - of the Admiralty of all things. They used the code word 'tank' to describe their designs in order to confuse German spies, who might think that they were designing water tanks! The first tank (September 1915) was called 'Little Willie'. The second model, called 'Big Willie', so impressed army chiefs that they ordered a hundred of them. (The French began to

develop a tank of their own at about the same time.)
Big Willie came in two versions, both heavily
armoured. The male version had guns and the
66 female version had **machine guns**. Early tanks
communicated with each other by metal semaphore*
arms or with flags. To communicate back to base they
sent carrier pigeons.

97 Tanks were first used in 1916 at the **Battle of the
Somme**, by the British. They got bogged down in the
mud. As it turned out this was a good thing because
the Germans decided that tanks were nothing to
worry about. Next year, when 378 Mark IV British
23 tanks trundled into the attack at the **Battle of
Cambrai**, the Germans were totally unprepared. The
massed tanks broke through three lines of German
trenches by mid-day. Cambrai was the beginning of
the end of trench warfare in France.

Early tanks were hideously uncomfortable. The only
light was a dim electric light bulb. The air inside was
infernally hot and the din from the engines was so
loud that men's eardrums sometimes split. When
machine gun bullets hit the outside, showers of
sparks were set off inside. Crews wore metal helmets
to protect themselves, with eye slits and chain mail to
cover their necks, like medieval knights-in-armour.

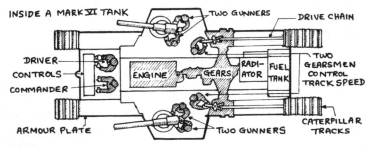

✗ Tannenberg, Battle of
where Hindenburg rose to fame

At the start of the war, while the Germans were
89 following their **Schlieffen Plan** and invading France,
the Russians invaded Germany from the east. The
German Eighth Army fell back before them through
East Prussia.

In August 1914
50 **Hindenburg** took
over as commander
of the Eighth Army
63 with **Ludendorff** as
his chief of staff.
Following plans
already worked
out, the Russians
were lured into a
trap and utterly
annihilated near
the town of

Tannenberg (now Stebark in Poland). During the
battle, the Russians used the new invention of radio
without first putting their messages into code, so the
Germans overheard everything the Russians
planned to do before they did it. 92,000 Russian
soldiers were taken prisoner and 30,000 were killed
or wounded, against just 13,000 German casualties.

Tannenberg launched the wartime careers of both
Hindenburg and Ludendorff. Germans began to
believe that the two men couldn't be beaten - a myth
which they both encouraged.

 transport ⚙

armies on the move

At the start of World War I, the only practical way to move things and people around was by train or by horse - and on foot. Camels and elephants had their uses in other parts of the world, but not in France where most fighting took place. Horses died by the hundred thousand during the war, many of them drowned in the mud of Flanders. Later, lorries began to be used.

British reinforcements arriving in France were shipped as near to the front as possible by rail. Men were crammed into passenger carriages or freezing cattle trucks - whatever was available. Dumped at the railhead, they then marched the final stage of their journey with enormously heavy packs on their backs. The march was so tough that some of them died before they reached the front.

Considering that it took a thousand railway carriages to move a division of 12,000 men with all their equipment, and that there was no other way to transport big guns or tanks, railways were vital. So vital that sections of track in England were torn up and sent to France to build military supply tracks,

107 usually light railways joining the **trenches** to existing French railheads.

66 Railways, like **machine guns**, favoured the defenders. Defenders could bring up supplies from behind their lines quite quickly by rail; attackers, once they moved forward from their own lines, were separated from their railheads so that supplies took a long time to reach them. This slowed down the speed of attacks. On top of that, most European countries ran their trains on different widths of track, so it was impossible to run your own trains outside your own borders unless you laid special lines for them first.

AUSTRIAN RAIL-ADAPTED MOTOR LORRY

🥾 trench fever ✏️
flu-like fever which infested trenches

107 The squalid, damp conditions of the **trenches** in France made them ideal breeding grounds for disease. Trench fever was first diagnosed in 1915 and affected huge numbers of men. It was caused by a virus and carried from one man to the next by lice, or 'chats', which infested the men's uniforms. One way

to control them was to run a lighted match up the seams of a shirt or jacket. The symptoms of trench fever were similar to very severe flu. About 5% of the victims never really got better.

BODY LOUSE (PEDICULUS HUMANUS)

🥾 trench foot 💉

fungus foot by another name

Trench foot is caused by a microscopic fungus which thrives in cold damp conditions. The muddy 107 **trenches** of northern France were ideal. At its worst, infected feet can swell up to three times their normal size and the foot loses all sense of touch - so that you can 'run a bayonet through it'. If left untreated, the foot may become gangrenous (rotten) and has to be cut off. The first cases were spotted among soldiers of 19 the **BEF** in 1914. During that winter, 20,000 British soldiers suffered from it. Trench conditions improved slightly in 1915 so there was less of the disease from then on, although it was always a serious problem.

🥾 trench warfare

digging in

67 After the **Battle of the Marne** in September 1914, the war in the west got stuck in the mud. The opposing armies settled down to face each other along five hundred miles of trenches which ran from the Swiss border to the English Channel. The standard trench system on both sides consisted of a forward trench connected to support and reserve trenches behind it by communications passages. Still further back were the artillery positions. In 1915, the Germans invented 'defence in depth' - several systems of trenches with two to three kilometres of land between them. If the

enemy broke through the first system, they still had to break through the next.

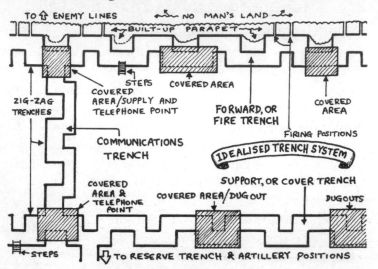

The trenches zigzagged as a protection against blast and to give the defenders good fields of fire against attackers. On the side of the trench facing the enemy there was usually a slight rampart and below that a 'firestep' so that men stepped up to fire but usually could walk around upright otherwise. Since it was dangerous to show your head above the parapet, observers often watched the enemy through periscopes. At short intervals there were bunkers or dugouts, a bit like caves, which offered protection against the weather and against enemy artillery fire. Radio was in its infancy, so communication between trenches was mainly by field telephone. Trench systems were strung with primitive telephone lines.

In front of the trenches, a thick hedge of barbed wire waited to entangle any attackers. At the beginning, single strands were hung with tin cans and the barbed wire was only meant to give warning of attack, but soon the whole front was festooned with thick barbed wire barricades, carefully placed so as to channel attackers into killing zones.

Because trenches were below ground level, there was nowhere lower for water to drain into. When it rained even the rats took cover. It was quite common for rats to try to join the men in their bunkers. Dampest of all were the trenches scraped out of the Flanders mud in 1914 by the **BEF**.

CUTAWAY OF AN ALLIED TRENCH

FRENCH SOLDIER →

WOODEN SHORING HOLDS UP SIDES

FIRE STEP (FOR SHOOTING FROM)

LADDERS

WOODEN DUCKBOARD PLANKS

DRAIN CHANNEL (USUALLY INEFFECTIVE)

19

107

These were usually flooded, and 'duck boards' laid along the trench bottoms as flooring were almost useless. The men suffered epidemics of **trench foot** and other diseases. Disease was inevitable. The earth and air were foul from more than a million rotting corpses, corpses which were buried, flung to the surface by artillery fire and reburied many times before the war itself was over.

Apart from the big battles, trench warfare tended to settle down to a routine. 'Stand to' was usually half an hour before sunrise, at which time platoons assembled on the fire step and sentries were posted. Then the men had breakfast. After that the day was taken up with routine chores. There was another 'stand to' at dusk when the day was over. Standard British procedure was for men to spend one week in the firing line, one week in the support trench and one week in the reserve trench, with a week behind the lines to recover.

~➣ VADs ♀
(Voluntary Aid Detachments)
brave women medics

VADs (Voluntary Aid Detachments) were made up of girls who came mostly from the middle and upper classes. They provided 23,000 nurses and 15,000 hospital orderlies to the medical services during the war. It was hard work for girls who'd led sheltered and privileged lives until that time. Their duties might include among other horrible things: taking the lice from the uniforms of wounded soldiers, changing bandages which reeked of pus, and helping to remove baskets full of amputated limbs. Many of these upper class girls discovered that they preferred to treat the ordinary soldiers rather than the officers, because the ordinary soldiers were less stuffy and more friendly. The girls' living conditions near to the field hospitals could be very uncomfortable. One girl described sleeping in her clothes in winter, because if she didn't, they were too stiff with frost in the morning for her to be able to put them on.

⚔ Verdun, Battle of
'The Grinding Machine'
terrible battle where the French stood their ground

38 **General von Falkenhayn**, Chief of Staff of the German armies at the start of the war, believed in 16 **attrition**. He decided to 'bleed France white' by attacking where the French would have to defend their land, at whatever the cost in French lives. He chose the fortress system of Verdun in northeast France because it was very important to the French and also because it threatened German positions.

The Germans attacked with a million men on 21 February 1916 after an artillery barrage of a million shells. At first there were only 200,000 French defenders, but these 200,000 held out - just. The Germans pushed them back to within a few kilometres of the main fortress. Almost surrounded, and despite the massive German force ranged against them, the French kept on fighting through the spring and into August under their commander 75 **Henri Pétain**. There was only one road in and out of the main fortress, along with a single light railway, and both were under almost constant German artillery fire. The road, known as the 'Voie Sacrée' (Sacred Way) by the French, became a lifeline for the French defenders. Each week up to 90,000 soldiers and their supplies could pass along it.

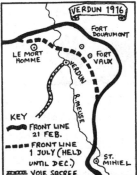

Verdun became known as the 'grinding machine'. Fighting was so fierce that men had to be replaced at regular intervals or they would have gone mad with the stress of it - as many did. By the end, most of the French army had fought at Verdun at some stage during the battle, which was the longest and bloodiest of the entire war. By the time it ended in December 1916, the French had suffered over 400,000 casualties and the Germans around 350,000. The French had not been 'bled white' - not quite.

Versailles, Treaty of
it brought peace - for a while

The Hall of Mirrors in the Palace of Versailles is a beautiful, light room, designed for the French king Louis XIV in the late seventeenth century. It was there that the final peace treaty of World War I, the Treaty of Versailles, was signed by representatives of the **Allies** and of Germany on 28 June 1919. The treaty was the result of weeks of hard talking at a Peace Conference earlier that spring led by the

11

62
30
116

big four: **Lloyd George**, **Georges Clemenceau**, **Woodrow Wilson** and Vittorio Orlando, Prime Minister of Italy. Germany, as loser of the war, had to shut up and listen.

Clemenceau wanted to stop any chance of Germany invading France ever again. Germany's army was to be limited to 100,000 men, she was forbidden to build various heavy armaments and her army had to stay out of the industrial Rhineland in the south of Germany. Also, Germany lost her overseas colonies and large areas of land in Europe. But what caused the most bitterness in Germany was that the German government was forced to agree that Germany had caused the war. As the one who started it, Germany now had to pay heavy 'reparations' for all the damage that the war had caused. Total reparations to the Allies came to an impossible sum of money - calculated at $300 billion in 1921. Bitterness about reparations was one of the main reasons for the rise of the German Nazi party in the 1930s and thus to World War II.

✕ Vittorio Veneto, Battle of
Italians on top

While France, Britain and Germany were slugging it out in northern France, a separate but connected struggle went on along the border between Italy, one
11 of the **Allies**, and the Austro-Hungarian Empire, one
27 of the **Central Powers**. In October 1918, when the Central Powers were weakening (Germany asked for
12 **armistice** on 3 October), Italy seized the moment to attack.

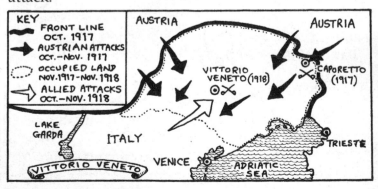

The Battle of Vittorio Veneto started on 23 October. Soon after, Italian troops, with some British assistance, crossed the River Piave near the Italian-Austrian border under cover of darkness and fog. Italian reserves poured after them and Austrian resistance crumbled. What was the point of them fighting and dying if Austria had already lost the war? Mutinies broke out in the Austrian and Hungarian regiments. By 30 October the Italians had taken, or rather retaken, the small Italian hill town of

 Vittorio Veneto and the battle was all but won. The Italians had captured 300,000 prisoners and the Austrians were begging for peace. The war in the south of Europe was finally over.

Western Front

'Western Front' is the name given to the main battle ground of World War I, which stretched nearly five hundred miles across northern France from the Swiss border to the English Channel. The Front hardly moved after the

67 **Battle of the Marne** in September 1914, when both sides dug in and

107 **trench warfare** began.

🚫 White Feather Movement
a cross admiral's bright idea

The White Feather Movement was launched in Folkestone in 1915 by a short-tempered British admiral called Penrose Fitzgerald. Many volunteer soldiers had been killed on the **Western Front** and there was a general feeling in Britain that the army was running out of men. The Movement encouraged small groups of women to waylay able-bodied men and to hand them a white feather - as a badge of cowardice. This was very unpopular with the soldiers who were doing the actual fighting. They might be handed white feathers when home on leave or even if they had been invalided away from the front. Other hapless victims included men who hadn't been allowed to join the army even though they'd tried - men such as miners, whose work was too important to the war effort for them to be allowed to join up. The White Feather Movement finally died down in 1918.

👑 Wilhelm II, Kaiser
nasty man - big moustache
1859-1941

If any one person can be held responsible for World War I, Kaiser Wilhelm is the man. He was a grandson of the British Queen Victoria and thus a cousin of

George V, but although related to the British Royal Family, he loathed the British. He was a vain, stupid and nasty man. He had a big moustache which was waxed every morning by his special barber, and a withered left arm. He liked to hurt people with his extra-strong handshake (with his right hand naturally).

Before the war, Wilhelm spent money like water on the German armed services, but once war began he turned out to be a weak leader. Power slipped from his hands to the army leaders, in particular to **Hindenburg** and **Ludendorff**. While German soldiers suffered and died, Wilhelm moved from palace to palace (he had seventy-six of them), hunting, sawing wood (his favourite hobby) and holding champagne, victory dinners. At the end of the war the **Allies** made him abdicate*. He ended his days in Holland where he was protected from a war crimes trial by his fellow monarch, Queen Wilhelmina.

⁵⁰⁶³

¹¹

Wilson, President Woodrow
he took America into the war

1856-1924

In 1914 President Woodrow Wilson declared that the USA was neutral - that it would not fight on either side, and he was re-elected in 1916 on the slogan: 'He kept us out of the war'. Meanwhile Germany became increasingly unpopular with the American public, especially after a German submarine sank the British liner *Lusitania* in May 1915, with the loss of 1,198

⁶⁵

people including 128 Americans. On 9 January 1917 the Germans declared unrestricted submarine warfare on all ships sailing to and from Britain, including American ships, and on 2 April 1917, under Wilson's leadership, America joined the war on the side of the **Allies**.

🥾 *Wipers Times*
a trenchant paper

Newspapers were produced by frontline troops in all the major armies. The *Wipers Times* (Ypres Times) is perhaps the best known. It was produced by men of the Sherwood Foresters from a run-down office somewhere near the **trenches** at Ypres. The first issue came out on 12 February 1916. It was produced under a string of different names for the rest of the war. Trench newspapers specialised in gossip and irreverent humour such as:

Question: what's a sure cure for optimism?
Answer: an artillery barrage.

⊘ **women working** ♀
an explosive idea

During the war, so many men joined the armed forces that there weren't enough of them left to keep the factories going and to farm the land. Women were asked to replace them. By the end of the war, there were 5 million women in full time work, 1.5 million of them doing jobs formerly done by men. 'Conductorettes' worked on the trams and buses, 'munitionettes' worked in the armaments factories,

'canaries' (so called because their skin went yellow from the chemicals) packed explosives into shells - a dangerous job. 240,000 women joined the Women's Land Army. They wore men's clothes for convenience, and along with prisoners of war and
31 **conscientious objectors**, they drove tractors and operated heavy machinery.

In the armaments factories, working class women earned good money, really for the first time. 'Munitionettes' were often criticised for spending their wages on pretty clothes, make-up - and drink. The fashion was for shorter skirts and shorter hair (so that it didn't get caught in factory machinery). Women were freer. They began to smoke in public.

Meanwhile, due to complaints from women, the factories started to provide proper toilets and cloakrooms, often for the first time.The war helped women in other countries as well. Millions of them took paid work in France and Germany, and in Russia, after the Russian Revolution, women were given total equal rights with men. In Turkey young army officers encouraged them to take off their veils and to go out to work - revolutionary in an Islamic country at that time.

✦ women's auxiliary services ♀
they helped the soldiers and sailors

More than 100,000 British women joined the women's auxiliary services during the war, taking on many non-fighting jobs in order to release men for the actual fighting. Most were employed in the WAACs, the Women's Auxiliary Army Corps, formed in 1917. Life for 'les Tomettes', as the WAACs were sometimes called, was often rough - and could be dangerous if they came under enemy artillery fire. The next most popular service was the WRNS, the Women's Royal Naval Service. The WRAF, the Women's Royal Air Force, was smallest because air warfare was still a new thing.

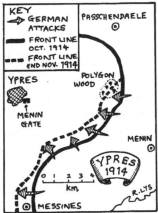

W.R.A.F. UNIFORM
(1918)

✗ Ypres, First Battle of
yet another slogging match

67 After the **Battle of the Marne** in September 1914, the Germans turned their attention away from the Paris region and back to southern Belgium. The First Battle of Ypres really got under way when the Germans launched another all-out attack on the small Belgian town of Ypres on 15 October. By 1 November they had taken

KEY
⇒ GERMAN ATTACKS
━ FRONT LINE OCT. 1914
▬▬▬ FRONT LINE END NOV. 1914

PASSCHENDAELE ◉

YPRES

POLYGON WOOD

MENIN GATE

MENIN ◉

YPRES 1914

0 1 2 3 4 km

R. LYS

◉ MESSINES

the Messines Ridge to the south of the town and came within a cat's whisker of breaking through British lines blocking the route from Menin to the southeast. By 22 November, the worst of the fighting had faded out due to bad weather and the two sides

107   settled down to **trench warfare**. The Germans

11   suffered 135,000 casualties during the battle and the **Allies**, mainly British, 75,000. British soldiers who died defending Ypres are remembered in the Menin Gate memorial in the town.

⚔ Ypres, Second Battle of

A German attack on the area around the town of Ypres in April and May 1915. The only major German attack on the western front that year. It's

45   notorious for being the battle when poison **gas** was used for the first time.

⚔ Ypres, Third Battle of
also known as 'Passchendaele'
hell in the mud

In June 1917, the Messines Ridge south east of the small town of Ypres, in Flanders in southern Belgium, was held by the Germans. Twenty tunnels were dug out from the British lines towards the ridge at a depth of around thirty metres. One was discovered, but the rest opened into chambers

107   directly beneath the German **trenches**. These were packed with 600 tons of high explosive. At 3.10 am on 7 June, the 'mines' were set off in a massive explosion which could be heard 209 km (130 miles) away in London. 10,000 Germans were killed

instantly and roughly the same number were stunned or injured. The next moment the British infantry stormed forward. The Messines Ridge was theirs by 6.00 am.

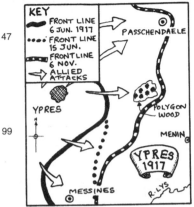

Encouraged by this success, **Douglas Haig** decided to launch a major attack in Flanders in southern Belgium, with the aim of capturing a number of German **submarine** bases on the Belgian coast. This attack is known as the Third Battle of Ypres, or 'Passchendaele' for short, after a small village captured by the British at the very end of it. Haig ignored warnings of heavy rain during August. Before his big attack started on 31 July, the British **artillery** launched a two week 'preliminary barrage' of 4.5 million shells which in the wet conditions had the effect of churning the battlefield into a sea of mud - and it didn't destroy the concrete German **machine gun** posts, or 'pill boxes' as they were called. When the British finally advanced, they did so through mud so deep that in places men and horses drowned in it.

When the battle finally fizzled out, after the British had taken the ruined village of Passchendaele to the east of Ypres, Haig had gained about ten kilometres (six miles) - and had lost 325,000 men.

GLOSSARY

ABDICATE: a monarch who abdicates gives up the throne.

CIVILIANS: civilians are all the people who do *not* serve in the armed forces of a country.

COMMUNISTS: communists believe that all means of 'production, distribution and exchange' (which means pretty well everything in an economy from factories to shops) should be owned and controlled by the public and the people who work in them.

JESUITS: Jesuits are an order of the Roman Catholic Church organised on semi-military lines and dedicated to spreading Catholicism, although they don't do any fighting.

KNOTS: knots are speed measured as nautical miles per hour, as opposed to ordinary miles per hour. One knot is roughly the same as 1.15 mph. In the old days, sailors used to let out a length of knotted rope behind their ships and reckoned their speed by the number of knots which ran over the side of the ship in a given time.

PACIFISTS: Pacifists are against going to war to settle arguments between countries. Extreme pacifists refuse to have anything at all to do with war.

PATRIOTISM: a patriot is someone who loves his or her country.

SEMAPHORE: a way of signalling using flags, arms or signal arms. Each sign means a letter of the alphabet.

INDEX

Africa 95
airships 8-9
Aisne, Second Battle of 27
Albert I 9-10
Allenby, General Sir
  Edmund 10-11,38,60,97
Allies 11,12,13,26,44,46,48,
  49,56,72,85,86,97,98,112,
  113,116,117,120
Angels of Mons 12
ANZACs 44
Arab Revolt 59
Armistice 7,12-13,41,49,
  74,88,113
Arras, Battle of 7,13-14
artillery 13,14-15,17,24,76,
  97,98,107,108,109,111,
  121
Asquith, Herbert Henry 16,
  29,33,52,62
attrition 14,16,111

Balkans 95
balloons 8,17-18,24
Beatty, Sir David 54
BEF see British
  Expeditionary Force
Big Bertha 15
blackout 18
Bolsheviks 19,71

Brest-Litovsk, Treaty of 19
British Expeditionary Force
  10,13,19-20,43,47,48,58,
  67,69,72,73,107,109
British Legion 20-1,48
Brittain, Vera 21
Brooke, Rupert 22,74
Brusilov Offensive 23
Brusilov, General Aleksey
  23

Cambrai, Battle of 7,23-4,
  103
Casement, Sir Roger
  David 25,36
causes of the war 25-6
Cavell, Edith Louisa 26
Central Powers 11,26,27,
  85,113
Chemin des Dames,
  Battle of 7,27-8
Christmas Truce 28-9
Churchill, Winston 11,
  29-30,34,40,43,45,96,102
Clemenceau, Georges 30,
  112
communists 19
conscientious objectors
  31-2,118
conscription 31,33

convoys **33-4**,63
Crécy, Battle of 12

Dardanelles 29,30,40,**43-5**
Day of Remembrance
12-13
doing your bit 35-6
Dreadnought 32

Easter Rising 6,25,**36-7**
Eastern Front 37
Edward VII 47
Etaples 37-8

Falkenhayn, Erich von 38,
51,111
Far East 96
Feisal Ibn Hussein 59
field hospitals 39
Fisher, Admiral John 39
Fitzgerald, Admiral Penrose
115
flu epidemic 40
Foch, Marshal Ferdinand
12,**41**
Fokker, Anthony 81
Franz Ferdinand,
Archduke 6,**41-2**,95
Franz Joseph I, Emperor
42
French, Sir John 20,**43**,48,
69

Gallipoli 22,**43-5**,85,95,96
gas 45-6,120

George V 35,**47**,115
Giffard, Henri 8

Haig, Sir Douglas 21,43,
47-8,63,121
Hindenburg Line 23,27,
48-9
Hindenburg, Paul von 6,
38,**50-1**,56,64,104,116
Hitler, Adolf 51,76

Impressionists 31
internment camps 52

James, Henry 22
Jehovah's Witnesses 32
Jellicoe, Sir John 52-3,55
Jesus 11
Joffre, Joseph 72
Jutland, Battle of 6,**53-5**,93

Kaiserschlacht 7,**56**
Kitchener armies 20,37,
57-8
Kitchener, Herbert 16,37,
57-8,**58-9**
Kluck, Alexander von 67
Kut, Siege of 96

Lawrence, T.E. 10,**59-60**
Leighton, Roland 21
Lenin, Vladimir Ilyich 19
live and let live 60-2
Lloyd George 16,29,30,34,
43,53,**62-3**,72,82,112

Louis XIV 112
Ludendorff, Erich von 6,48, 49,50,51,56,**63-4**,104,116
Lusitania 6,**65**,116

machine guns 11,13,24,49, **66-7**,78,98,103,106,121
Marne, First Battle of 6, **67-8**,69,90,107,114,119
Menin Gate memorial 120
Mesopotamia 96
Messines 14,120,121
Mills bombs 69
Mons, Battle of 6,12,**69**, 73,84
mortars 70
mutinies 28,56,72,114

Nicholas II, Czar 19,59,**71**
Nivelle Offensive 7,13,27, 72,76
Nivelle, General Robert 13,27,28,**72**
no man's land 13,28,61, 66,**72-3**
nurses 25,39,110

Old Contemptibles 73
Omdurman, Battle of 58
Orlando, Vittorio 112
Owen, Wilfrid 22,**73-4**,88

pacifists 31
pal's battalions 74-5,99
Palestine 10,97

Paris Commune 31
Passchendaele 63,120-1
Pétain, Henri-Philippe 28, 72,**75-6**,111
planes 9,24,67,**76-81**,83
Poincaré, Raymond 31
preliminary bombardment 14,15,24,121
Princip, Gavrilo 41,42

radio 17,77,104,108
rationing 63,**81-2**
reparations 113
Richthofen, Manfred von 77,**83**
rifles 62,69,**83-4**,98
Robertson, Sir William 16
Romania 97
Russian Revolution 7,56, 118

Salonika 85-7,95
Samson, Spicer 95
Sassoon, Siegfried 22,32, 74,**87-8**
Scapa Flow 88-9
Scheer, Reinhardt 55
Schlieffen Plan 68, **89-90**,104
Schlieffen, Alfred Graf von 89
Schweiger, Walter 65
shell shock 88,**90-1**
ships 53,**91-4**
side shows 94-7

Somme, First Battle of
7,16,48,75,**97-9**,103
spies 26
submarines 6,18,25,33,
34,64,65,81,88,94,
99-101,117,121
suffragettes 101-2

tanks 7,24,29,35,**102-3**
Tannenberg, Battle of 6,
50,64,**104**
Territorial Force 58
torpedoes 94,99
transport 105-6
trench fever 106
trench foot 107,109
trenches 13,28,49,60,66,
68,69,70,72,83,86,102,
106,**107-10**,114,117,120

U-boats *see* submarines

VADs *see* **Voluntary Aid
Detachments**
Verdun, Battle of 6,7,9,16,
38,51,72,75,98,**111-12**
Versailles, Treaty of 112-3
Victoria, Queen 115
Vimy Ridge 13
**Vittorio Veneto, Battle of
113-4**
**Voluntary Aid
Detachments** 21,39,**110**

Western Front 114,115

**White Feather Movement
115**
Wilhelm II, Kaiser 51,73,
115-6
Wilhelmina, Queen 116
Wilson, Woodrow 112,
116-7
Wipers Times **117**
women 35,62,101,110,
117-8
**women's auxiliary
services 119**

Ypres, First Battle of 6,
119-20
Ypres, Second Battle of
45,**120**
Ypres, Third Battle of
7,48,63,**120-1**

Zeppelin, Count Ferdinand
von 8
zeppelins 8,9

Now Read On

If you want to know more about World War I, see if your local library or bookshop has either of these books.

ALL ABOUT THE FIRST WORLD WAR
By Pam Robson (Hodder Wayland, 2002).
This book is ideal for an 'at-a-glance' overview of World War I. It tracks the progress of the battles and investigates how peace was finally achieved. The timeline, glossary and clearly-headed spreads make it easy to refer to essential dates, facts and personalities. Maps, contemporary photography, paintings, posters and pictures of artefacts all help bring the topic to life.

WHAT THEY DON'T TELL YOU ABOUT WORLD WAR I
Also by Bob Fowke (Hodder Headline 2001). Bob Fowke tells the story of the War simply and clearly. He finds some humour in it where there's humour to be found but never glosses over the tragedy. This book is an excellent introduction to the War.

ABOUT THE AUTHOR

Bob Fowke is a popular author of children's information books. Writing under various pen names and with various friends and colleagues, he has created many unusual and entertaining works on all manner of subjects.

There's always more to his books than meets the eye - look at all the entries in the index of this one!

Who? What? When?
ORDER FORM

0 340 85185 6	TUDORS	£4.99
0 340 85184 8	VICTORIANS	£4.99
0 340 85186 4	WORLD WAR I	£4.99
0 340 85187 2	WORLD WAR II	£4.99

All Hodder Children's books are available at your local bookshop or newsagent, or can be ordered direct from the publisher. Just write to the address below. Prices and availability subject to change without notice.

Hodder Children's Books, Cash Sales Department, Bookpoint, 130 Milton Park, Abingdon, Oxon, OX14 4SB, UK.
Email address: orders@bookpoint.co.uk

Please enclose a cheque or postal order made payable to Bookpoint Ltd to the value of the cover price and allow the following for postage and packing:
UK & BFPO - £1.00 for the first book, 50p for the second book, and 30p for each additional book ordered, up to a maximum charge of £3.00. OVERSEAS & EIRE - £2.00 for the first book, £1.00 for the second book, and 50p for each additional book.

If you have a credit card you may order by telephone - (01235) 400414 (lines open 9am-6pm, Monday to Saturday; 24 hour message answering service). Alternatively you can send a fax on 01235 400454.